AL-QAEDA IN THE ISLAMIC MAGHREB

SHADOW OF TERROR OVER THE SAHEL
FROM 2007

AL J. VENTER

Photographs by Yann Peducasse
Regiment d'Hélicoptres de Combat

Pen & Sword

First published in Great Britain in 2018 by
PEN AND SWORD MILITARY
an imprint of
Pen and Sword Books Ltd
47 Church Street
Barnsley
South Yorkshire S70 2AS

Photos courtesy of Yann Peducasse unless otherwise stated
Maps by George Anderson
Typeset by Aura Technology and Software Services, India
Printed and bound in Malta by Gutenberg

ISBN 978 1 526728 73 9

Pen & Sword Books Ltd incorporates the imprints of Pen & Sword
Archaeology, Atlas, Aviation, Battleground, Discovery, Family History, History, Maritime, Military,
Naval, Politics, Railways, Select, Social History, Transport, True Crime, Claymore Press, Frontline
Books, Leo Cooper, Praetorian Press, Remember When, Seaforth Publishing and Wharncliffe.

For a complete list of Pen and Sword titles please contact
Pen and Sword Books Limited
47 Church Street, Barnsley, South Yorkshire, S70 2AS, England
email: enquiries@pen-and-sword.co.uk
website: www.pen and-sword.co.uk

CONTENTS

List of Maps

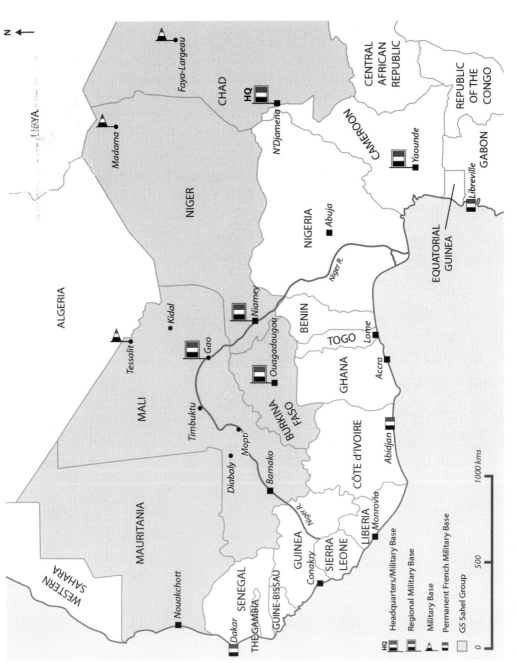

The French in West Africa.

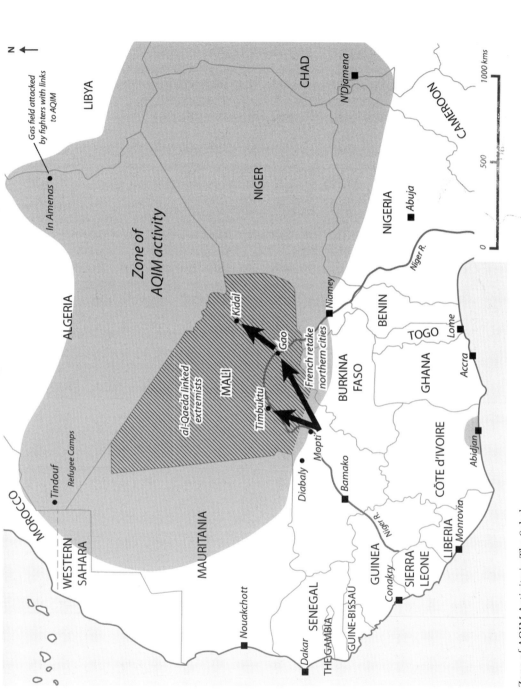

Zone of AQIM Activity in The Sahel.

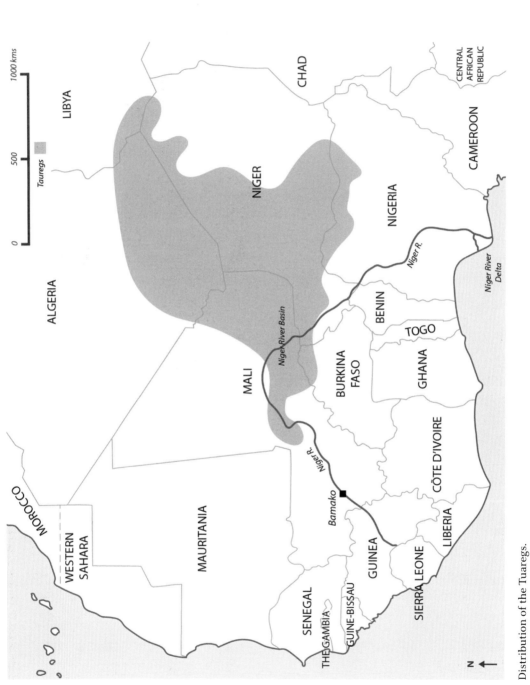

Distribution of the Tuaregs.

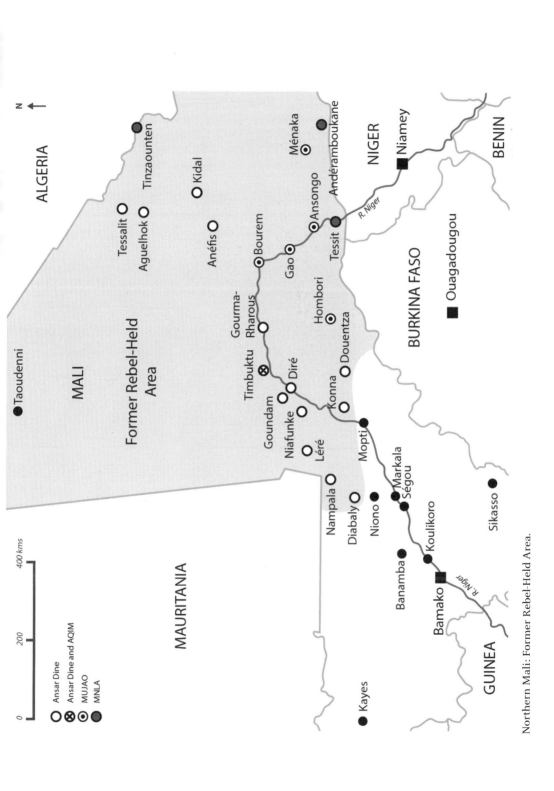

Northern Mali: Former Rebel-Held Area.

A Tuareg at Tessalit in the north after French troops had occupied the town.

INTRODUCTION

I have a great personal interest in the wars and insurrections currently being waged in parts of Africa, many linked to al-Qaeda. The most prominent—and for a while, certainly the most effectual of these conflicts—was launched in Mali by AQIM, an acronym for al-Qaeda in the Islamic Maghreb, in 2012. Unlike other African wars of recent decades, it is not yet over. Nor has it been compounded by the so-called Clausewitzian factors of 'fog, friction, unpredictability and chance'.

What the French did was basic: Paris, in short shrift, made the fundamental decision to go into Mali in force, in large part to prevent that country from becoming a 'Failed State' (a phrase many contemporary commentators are rather fond of). France then mustered or put on standby the forces likely to be involved. Perhaps a day or two later the order came down from the top and the French army and air force went in. Only then did the Élysée Palace advise its allies, including the United States, that the game was on.

Perhaps three weeks later the majority of the jihadists responsible for all these troubles had been driven out of most of Mali's northern cities and towns and the French army—with the help of several dozen other countries—set about systematically consolidating

Bamako, a modern progressive city on the vast Niger river.

the situation in this troubled West African nation. It was notable that one of AQIM favourite ploys of kidnapping French nationals stopped almost immediately.

Was the campaign a success? After roughly ten weeks in the field the French had seven of their men killed in action; the enemy lost something like half of their estimated strength of about 2,000 fighters, perhaps considerably more.

France's African allies in this war—the armies of Chad, Niger, Burkina Faso, Senegal and several others—suffered losses too, the majority in later stages of the campaign as a result of AQIM's carefully considered last resort: suicide bombings.

But, as has become a feature of quite a few of today's irregular struggles, which include Islamic State's machinations in Iraq and Syria, al-Shabaab in Somalia and Boko Haram in Nigeria, there have been far fewer soldiers killed since the insurrection started than the number of civilians killed: those losses run to four figures.

As a journalist, documentary producer and author, I covered the region for decades. My peregrinations have taken me by road, air, motor bike, *taxi brousse*, boat, ship, Mammy wagon and very occasionally by bike and pirogue, all the way from St Louis, France's first colonial naval base in the region north of Dakar, to Somalia and the Indian Ocean on the far side of the African continent. From the mid-1960s, apart from being resident in Nigeria for a while, there were many visits to the northern half of Africa. My trips included just about all former British and French possessions along the way—as well as one or two that were either Spanish or Portuguese. At one stage, I ended up in the Sudan making another TV doccie.

A desert scene on the outskirts of Timbuktu. (Photo ICRC)

Khartoum is not a happy memory, though seminal to this book because Osama bin Laden—who created the ogre we have come to refer to as al-Qaeda—initiated his struggle against the West from the Sudan. One of his first actions was to organize an assassination attempt on Egyptian president Hosni Mubarak who was visiting Addis Ababa at the time.

This former Saudi national—he was eventually disowned by the Riyadh regime—first flew to Sudan from Afghanistan in 1991, the fledgling al-Qaeda terror grouping having been formed three years before. At that stage, officially at least, the U.S. still considered bin Laden a friendly mujahidin. By 1998, less than two years after he was expelled from Sudan, he had become America's most wanted man, thanks to the truck bombings of U.S. embassies in Nairobi and Dar es Salaam that left 224 people dead. It seems reasonable to conclude that his years in the Sudan were crucial to the development of his terrorist network, which was eventually to spawn AQIM.

For most of the five years that bin Laden lived in the Sudan, he stayed in a pink and beige, brick-and-stucco three-storey house on Al-Mashtal Street in the affluent Al-Riyadh quarter of Khartoum, something the CIA knew all about. There were quite a few requests to the Office of the President from Langley to 'take him out', but apart from the invasion of Iraq, George W. Bush was a milquetoast compared to the Republican head of state not long before him, Ronald Reagan. That Bush the Younger ordered a few cruise missiles to be fired at a factory on the outskirts of Khartoum that was involved with chemical weapon precursors, was regarded at the time by both friends and enemies as a sop to

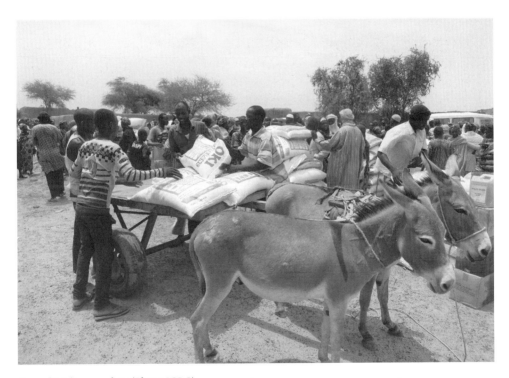

A rural Malian market. (Photo ICRC)

French troops boarding a USAF Boeing C-17 Globemaster III at Istres, France, January 2013.

counter further criticism. Certainly, he could have nipped the fledgling terror movement in the bud, but he chose not to.

My own visit coincided with a period of strong ties between the Sudan and the Soviets and on my second morning in Khartoum I was arrested by a group of soldiers for taking a photo of my hotel and then marched at gunpoint through dusty streets to the city's central police station. I spent several hours trying to explain to a bunch of officials that I was a British journalist and not a spy. Worse, my official-looking *Daily Express* press card achieved absolutely no sway with those fuzzy-brained interlocutors. Getting nowhere, they eventually relented and I was allowed to return to my hotel, this time unescorted. In retrospect, I suppose it could have been worse: the Sudan seems always to have been a malevolent place, having hosted the world's longest series of wars which have gone on since the 1950s.

For all that, Africa in those distant days was arguably the most fascinating of all the continents in which to work as a foreign correspondent. Until then, apart from Kenya's Mau Mau emergency, Biafra, apartheid, the Congolese débâcle and escalating troubles in Rhodesia, it seemed to have escaped the kind of drama we are witnessing today in the Middle East and parts of Asia. We all hoped that the great continent was finally emerging from its millennia-long slumber.

In this book I focus on what is presently taking place in some former French colonies in Africa. That region is commonly referred to as the Sahel, south of the Sahara Desert, though the French like to call it the Sahel-Sahara. Over time I was able to visit almost all those countries, though it is the Republic of Mali that concerns us here, even though every one of its neighbours has been involved in conflict over the past decade.

It is an expansive region. In fact, in this enormous stretch of the earth's surface—placed on the map of the United States, it would extend from San Francisco to the Ohio river—there are still only three north–south 'roads' noted on my Michelin map and they are the thinnest of lines placed over dotted tracks where the original caravan trails used to be. More to the point, there is not one that goes east to west and the great Sahara is as empty now as it has been through the centuries.

Nigeria comes rather sharply into focus in later chapters because I lived and worked there for a while. Africa's most populous country is obviously integral to the security equation of most of West Africa because a fairly substantive force of militant Boko Haram jihadists in the northeast of that former British colony has been active there for far too long. More pertinent, there seems very little the Nigerian army and air force have been able to do in order to tackle this problem at source. There was a stage, in 2015, when the Nigerians believed that a small group of professional soldiers from South Africa might possibly have an answer to this escalating insurgency. They did, and suddenly things began to change. That came after the Abuja government of West Africa's superpower secretly approached a group of former South African mercenaries to gather together a force and see whether they could sort out the mess. Nigeria did so knowing full well that South African law does not permit its nationals to fight in foreign wars. The people the Nigerians contacted were all linked to a now disbanded company with the unlikely name

French troops prepare for take-off, Istres, France, January 2013.

13

of Executive Outcomes, the same mercenary organization that ended the civil wars in Angola and Sierra Leone some years before. And since EO has an 'alumnae' network that stretches all the way across the African continent and remains strong today, the new combat unit—only seventy-five strong, including an air wing with helicopter gunships—was ready to roll within weeks. Their numbers included many former South African Defence Force personnel—black and white—quite a few of whom were already in their fifties and some even older. Almost all had previously been blooded in mercenary work in Angola and Sierra Leone. Most international news reports at the time spoke of a foreign force of several hundred, which was simply not true.

Effectively, said one of these hired guns, "I think the ghost of EO was resurrected. The Nigerian decision to hire our blokes to fight this new form of Islamist terror came at a good time and, actually, we did quite well." Though press coverage of that conflict was minimal, the international community—and many Nigerians—were stunned at how suddenly things turned around. This tiny group of mercenaries fought for only six months in northeastern Nigeria and in that short time achieved more than the Nigerian army had managed to do in six years of sporadic combat against a powerfully motivated Islamist force, not dissimilar to AQIM.

What has since emerged is that the South Africans had a secret. "When we go to war," one of my friends with whom I had been in Angola admitted, "we like to command the night." This was something that very rarely happened in Nigeria in the past, he disclosed, because many African tribal folk, particularly those in West and Central Africa, are susceptible to their own primitive superstitions about the hours of darkness. "We'd been in

French troops call for an air strike.

14

this situation before, in Sierra Leone, so when the sun set we left our secure bases and did our thing." It was apparently something for which Boko Haram was totally unprepared.

But then, six months later, South Africa's mercenary participation ended. Nigeria's new president Muhammadu Buhari, a former major-general in the Nigerian army was sworn in in late May 2015 and soon afterward the money intended to pay EO was stolen and the venture called to a halt. Buhari was not actually opposed to the mercenary effort because, officially, word was put out that it was Nigerian troops who were winning the war and not a rogue band of geriatric foreigners. The Nigerian military was obviously involved, but their troops played only a peripheral role supplying hardware like armoured vehicles and weapons, but little else. Their main problem apparently was that they were not geared or prepared for night deployments.

A couple of months later, all EO veterans returned home and there is an ongoing dispute as to whether everybody was properly paid. Since then, an impasse in hostilities has returned and Boko Haram is once again terrorizing civilians and kidnapping their daughters.

That insurgency is actually an extension of what has been taking place in Mali because Boko Haram and squads of AQIM irregulars are motivated by similar objectives. The difference is that AQIM did a better job of spreading both the message and inculcating terror in the minds of those affected when they launched their campaign prior to France stepping in. It is just as well that Paris reacted the way it did because the French, with strong support from its regional allies—including elements from both the Chad and

A French Tiger (or 'Tigre') gunship in Mali.

Nigerién military—soon halted the overt spread of a Salafist-orientated revolution. This subversive element has since moved underground.

Had the French not acted as they did, it is fairly certain that we could today be faced with the African equivalent of the Taliban ensconced in much of West Africa, with several more countries in that part of the world threatened with jihadist-inspired revolution.

It goes further. Both radical groups—Boko Haram and AQIM—though essentially following somewhat differing ideological paths, have declared an alliance of sorts, got their heads together when opportunities allowed abroad and offered support when needed. They also promised to jointly administer all of Africa once it was finally conquered by the faithful, as it is promulgated by their revolutionary imams: "In the name of Allah."

That day, were it ever to happen, is remote and is almost impossible to envisage because there are several hundred million moderate followers of the Muslim faith, African Christians, animists and others who stand firmly in their way.

A group of Islamic revolutionaries out of Chad attempted to overrun the Central African Republic (CAR), another French colony, in 2012. Though it took a while, the rebels were eventually stopped in their tracks by the French army and a spirited defence by African Union troops that included a few hundred South African soldiers that took on several thousand revolutionaries out of Chad in Bangui. After three days of fierce fighting, they eventually killed enough insurgents to curtail their thrust.

Most important, to the surprise of many, a sizeable sector of the Christian population also reacted, more often than not with the same measure of violence that the invaders

"Thank-you France."

had been dishing out. Thousands of people, on both sides of an invisible dividing line, perished in the process.

An immediate consequence of all these troubles is that present-day conflicts involving Islamist militants in much of this vast Sahellian region are not the kind of bloody military campaigns we have been witnessing in Iraq or Syria, or even the less intense struggle the Taliban is today waging in Afghanistan. Instead, Mali's attempted insurrection initially involved comparatively few combatants—people of Moorish, Arabic and some of Tuareg extraction—though within their ranks there were also quite a few disaffected soldiers from the regular Malian army who had thrown in their lot with the revolutionaries. To so many of them it seemed that AQIM offered real hope and a way of countering a government that was almost overwhelmingly corrupt. In this case, the rot had set in from the top a long time before.

Also involved were, and still are, Hausas, some Peuls (Fulanis in Nigeria), Songais, quite a few Libyans as well as Saudis and the rest, with the result that Mali's conflict, though low key compared to before, is still 'bubbling' as one local news sheet described it.

Jihadi militants discreetly emerge from time to time, attack a military outpost, lay an IED along a road or track they know is favoured by the military or, more commonly, use youngsters—boys and girls—to murder innocents in suicide bomb attacks. Occasionally these zealots are emboldened to enter a city or one of many popular tourist jaunts in any of these countries in desperate bids to leave an imprint.

Many times in the past four or five years they have succeeded in drawing blood, but invariably the perpetrators are killed in the process because the defenders have developed a few tricks of their own. Also, there are no set rules about how such things are done: these are low-key uprisings, this is Africa in the raw and something as mundane as Human Rights is rarely an issue.

It is worth mentioning that more often than not, both sides are guilty of excesses, usually under fire or the handling of prisoners. Those jihadists who are captured are customarily dealt with, kept alive only as long as they have information to impart. Then, quite simply, they disappear and there are no questions asked. There are thousands of tiny unmarked patches in the desert sand that hide the consequences of this attrition. Most of those executed would have been given the opportunity to reveal what they knew about their organizations or their revolutionary associates and, as I have seen for myself several times in other wars, true followers of the Faith rarely yield anything voluntarily.

There are several other aspects related to working in Africa today. For a start, several European journalists, men and women, have been murdered by the jihadists in the Sahel after agreeing to venture out, usually after dark, ostensibly to meet members of 'the other side'. These meetings were all organized by supposedly trusted 'friends' who gained the confidence of the news gatherers.

Tourists have also been targeted, most times to extort five- or six-figure ransoms. And while governments volunteer nothing about how much has been paid, and to whom, we are all aware that this kind of hostage-taking soon became extremely lucrative, at least until the French stepped in and collared some of the perps involved.

Another problem facing the contemporary journalist is that it is much more difficult for the average hack to get around in Africa these days. A quarter century or more ago the rule of law was the accepted norm by both friend and foe, but all that has changed for the worse: the water has become muddied, as it were.

Take a few examples, starting with the civil war in Sierra Leone a couple of decades ago. Cannibalism was a feature on both sides of the front lines and though it was not considered proper to write about it, we were very much aware that it happened.

Colonel Bert Sachse, who commanded Executive Outcomes contingents in that country in the mid-1900s, told me that he had a devil of a business getting government troops to surrender all the prisoners of war they had captured. Usually it was a case of keeping one or two of these poor sods to 'help with meals'. The colonel was dead serious: he explained that often enough he'd got word often that local units were holding prisoners, but when he sent a helicopter to fetch them for interrogation there was often one short.

The rebels, in contrast, were totally blunt about what they would do to any one of us if we were taken, dead or alive. Neall Ellis, Sierra Leone's lone mercenary aviator, was regularly getting messages passed on to him by the rebels that if his helicopter was to come down behind their lines, they would cut out his heart and eat it.[1]

They did exactly that to Bob MacKenzie, an American Vietnam veteran and mercenary who became the first white commander of the Sierra Leonean armed forces after the last of the British officers departed in the 1960s. In his first action against the rebels at Mile 93 (out of Freetown) in 1995, he was wounded and taken prisoner by what he would have referred to as 'gooks'. After being tortured to death the rebels cut out his heart and ate it, raw.[2]

According to a London *Daily Telegraph* report in January 2014, something similar was taking place in the troubles that descended on the Central African Republic. Only, being a former French colony, those involved were a bit more discreet about it.[3]

Another reality about contemporary reporting in Africa is that there are numerous forces at work that might do you harm were you to get too close to source, or possibly too intrusive. For instance, few journalists, white or black, have been able to gain access to some of the rebel groups active in the Niger Delta, and for very good reason. Those people are smashed half the time and certainly, prior to going into action, the majority of rebels bandying weapons about are as high as proverbial kites.

1. THE WAR IN WEST AFRICA

"The air force and air power must be regarded as political tools. For our political leaders, the ability of what we call first entry is vital. [When] we intervened [in Mali] we took on a lot of responsibility."

Lt-Gen Jean-Patrick Gaviard (Armée de l'Air)

When Operation Serval was launched in January 2013, it lasted eighteen months and became the fourth French military operation on the go in Africa at the time: also were Operation Licorne in the Côte d'Ivoire, or Ivory Coast (2002–14), Operation Épervier in Chad (1986–2014) and Burkina Faso's Operation Sabre (2012–14).

All were eventually incorporated under the mantle of a newly formed campaigned dubbed Operation Barkhane, a single, overall military command with headquarters in N'Djamena, the capital of the Chad Republic. More salient, the war in Mali—now active for several years—became the single biggest military campaign faced by France in Africa since the end of hostilities in Algeria half a century before.

Apart from being involved in a series of military operations in the Central African Republic, also jihadist-backed and emanating out of Chad (and which could have gone either way had Paris not stood fast), France remains committed to maintaining stability

The bridge across the Niger at Gao.

Some 300 refugees managed to cram onto this truck fleeing south. (Photo ICRC)

throughout the Sahel region farther northwestward. This is an enormous region which stretches several thousand kilometres from Senegal to Chad.

In its efforts to quell the violence, French forces are currently assisted by military components from of a number of international partners, the majority either European or African, though the United States makes significant contributions, both on the ground and in the air. Though all these exploits have been a drain on the French exchequer, it was fortuitous that in the AQIM-sponsored Malian upheaval, the French army and air force had both manpower as well as ground and air resources in place in several adjoining African countries that were called on at very short notice—literally hours—to provide back-up.

As it happened, the French air force operating out N'Djamena struck at several rebel targets on Friday, January 11, 2013 in an effort—successful as it transpired—to halt several groups of heavily armed Islamist fighters sweeping south toward Mali's capital Bamako. Independent projections made by strategists at the time, maintained that had this forceful action not been implemented—and with the Malian army in total disarray—the rebels might have reached the capital within two or three days. Simply put, there was almost nothing in their way to stop their revolutionary momentum.

Air strikes against columns of AQIM fighters and their Ansar al-Din and Movement for Tawhid and Jihad in West Africa (known by its French acronym MUJAO) continued for much of Saturday, January12, by which time French ground units were already heading north to confront them. That happened after the Malian army had lost control of the strategically important crossroads town of Konna, about seventy kilometres north of Mopti, also on the great river.

The next day, a communiqué released by French defence minister Jean-Yves Le Drian said rebels heading toward the central town of Mopti were attacked and that a French pilot had been killed in action. With French aircraft pounding Islamist rebels in Mali for a second day, neighbouring West African states hurriedly implemented plans to deploy their troops in an effort to prevent ancillary groups linked to al-Qaeda expanding their power base. That followed a warning by France that the control of northern Mali by the militants posed a serious security threat to Europe. Under cover of French fighter planes and attack helicopters, the Malian army rallied and returned to Konna to rout a rebel convoy, which effectively drove the Islamists out of the town. A senior army officer in Bamako said more than a hundred rebel fighters had been killed.

Once Paris had made the decision to go into what was clearly a new and escalating war, things started to move. French forces deployed included a company of the 21st Marine Infantry Regiment, an armoured cavalry platoon, a 'Foreign Cavalry Regiment' from the Legion and a company of infantry marines.

A day after the first retaliatory shots had been fired, a French light aviation unit transported Eurocopter Tiger HAP attack helicopters to Mali. From the Côte d'Ivoire came a company of the 3rd Marine Infantry Parachute Regiment together with troops from the 1st Parachute Hussar Regiment and the 17th Parachute Engineer Regiment, until then deployed as part of Operation Licorne. All departed Abidjan for Bamako in convoy formation followed by columns of VBCI infantry fighting vehicles, with the army making use of a fleet of low-loaders to transport their armour to the frontier with Mali. From there, the fighting vehicles proceeded independently.

Contact! Gunship crews dash to their helicopters.

Ground operations in this West African country were commanded by Brigadier-General Bernard Barrera, about whom we shall hear more a little later because he followed up his posting in Africa with *Operation Serval: Notes de Guerre—Mali 2013,* one of the best books to emerge from the war. That might be expected of the son of a veteran of the Algerian war, who, as his book readily proclaims, is steeped in his country's colonial military exploits. As Barrera recalled, having arrived in Bamako, he essentially had to start from scratch because Mali's national military infrastructure had been almost stripped bare. He was obliged to send his staff scavenging for transport vehicles, spare parts and satellite phones in local markets. As he recounts, even weeks into Operation Serval, many of his troops were still wearing heavy green uniform for want of desert fatigues.

The French air force too was inordinately busy. Its commanders initially deployed two Mirage F1s from Europe as well as six Mirage 2000D fighter jets, the latter already part of Operation Épervier in Chad. Additionally, three KC-135 Stratotankers as well as a single C-139 and a Transall C-160 from the French airbase in Chad were tasked with support roles.

On Monday January 13, four Dassault Rafale multi-role fighter jets flew in from the Daint-Dizier airbase in France—with air refuelling en route provided by American planes. Their role was to attack targets in the low-rise city of Gao, which, like several other Malian centres lies on the Niger river. It had originally been chosen by the insurgents as its central command headquarters for the southward onslaught.

The first real casualty of the war resulted from a surprise Special Forces attack on the outskirts of Mopti, which, by now, was firmly in the sights of the French high command. In one of the early firefights of the war, the French dispatched an army detachment by

Airlift of Gazelle helicopters to Mali.

French helicopter gunship over the Niger.

air from Burkina Faso, that base being part of the French regional counter-terrorism Operation Sabre.

According to reports published subsequently, the entire Malian army unit originally defending the city fled in every available vehicle they could grab as soon as they heard that al-Qaeda was headed their way. That left two Armée de l'Air Gazelle SA 342 gun-ships—not the most advanced version of today's sophisticated helicopters—as well as a modest force of special forces on the ground as the only barrier between the advancing AQIM jihadists and Bamako.

Lieutenant Damien Boiteux, the pilot of one of the Gazelles came under concerted ground fire and was hit, even though he and his wingman went in—as is customary in these operations—low and fast. While the second Gazelle was also hit, it was forced to make an emergency landing some distance from the area of operations. The crew was picked up soon afterward and the pilot's body subsequently recovered by the Special Forces squad. Boiteux was posthumously promoted to captain.

It was this action, and several others that took place at about the same time that caused a spokesman for the ministry of defence in Paris to declare: "Our enemies are well armed, well equipped and better trained than most rebel groups encountered so far." He conceded that the French military was surprised at the determined manner in which the rebels not only held ground but managed to counterattack.

In both Paris and Bamako the reality soon emerged that the jihadist guerrillas—armed with advanced military hardware, much of it brought overland in trucks across the Sahara

Gao airport in northern Mali had taken a severe battering before the French succeeded in ousting AQIM forces.

from Libya and supplemented with what they had seized from the fleeing Malian army—were a lot more aggressive and efficient than almost everybody had anticipated. Some of that evidence came to light after French troops and helicopter gunships surrounded the town of Diabaly, about 500 kilometres northeast of Bamako near the Algerian frontier. In the process the rebels—who had initially taken the town by force—were trapped.

Customarily, AQIM coalition forces—which include home-grown Ansar al-Din and MUJAO—would flee the scene after the first French aircraft had delivered their loads. But not this time. As French forces moved farther north, solid evidence of foreign jihadists fighting with the mainly Tuareg rebels emerged, including squads of trained children armed with AK-47s. It also became clear that one of the features of this war was that the enemy rarely took prisoners.

The Malian insurrection of January 2012 that led to French intervention a year later was not an isolated event. By then, several other African regions were starting to experience the influence of Islamic State, including Algeria, Mali, Burkina Faso and Libya as well parts of the Sudan and northern Chad (where it borders on Libya).

Most recently, Ansarul Islam (Defenders of Islam), emerged as the umbrella for all Islamist operations in northern Burkina Faso. BBC sources disclosed that this group is led by Ibrahim Malam Dicko, regarded by those involved with his exploits as "an extremely radical Imam".

Originally from that country's northern city of Djibo, Dicko has organized several strikes against civilian Burkina Faso targets, first in January 2017 and eight months later in Ouagadougou, where twenty civilians were cut down by automatic fire. An uncompromising radical with a military background, Dicko fought in Mali in the ranks of the MUJAO Islamist movement before he founded his own guerrilla force. After a brief spell in a Bamako jail following his arrest by foreign forces in 2013, he was released and wasted no time in returning home and launching his own jihad.

Algeria had remained a focus of dissident Islamic activity for many years where guerrilla involvement was, and occasionally still is, mostly drawn from the Algerian and local Saharan communities such as the Tuaregs and the Berabiche tribal clans of Mali as well as Moroccans. As we have seen, that outfit has also has links with both Nigeria's Boko Haram as well as Somalia's al-Shabaab.[1]

Officially, the main terror group active in these regions is known as the Organization of al-Qaeda in the Land of the Islamic Maghreb (Qaedat al-Jihad fi Bilad al-Maghrib al-Islami), customarily shortened to Al-Qaeda in the Islamic Maghreb (AQIM). It is also part of Al-Mourabitoun; Jama'at Nasr al-Islam wal Muslimin and its allies are Movement for Oneness and Jihad in West Africa, Africa, Ansura, Nigeria: all quite complicated, but potentially deadly because their objective is to achieve jihadist dominance at any cost.

Prior to January 2007 AQIM was known as the Salafist Group for Preaching and Combat. The French acronym is GSPC (Groupe Salafiste pour la Prédication et le Combat).[2] In a series of personal communications, Colonel Alain Bayle, the French military attaché in London, was of the opinion that AQIM had launched a 400-year war. Though fighting remained sporadic after the first AQIM thrusts, he reckoned that regions adjoining the

A gunner on a French infantry fighting vehicle in Mali.

Malian troops on the move prior to being airlifted northward for deployment against the rebels.

Sahara made conditions for containing this resolute group of rebels much more difficult than the original South East Asian war fought by a previous generation of Americans.

He also stressed that "this was not a [series of wars] only against Muslims but rather, against people having various interests in challenging the established order". He added that the Malian insurgency remained a classical guerrilla one, but warned, "It is taking much more than basic counterinsurgency efforts to contain it." For a start, he stated, the region in which AQIM operates covers several countries and is almost as big as Western Europe. "The enemy is elusive, clever and remarkably well trained, considering that these are people of the Sahel who have made an art of slipping in and out of mountain hide-aways with the kind of ease that comes with experience. Worse, in the beginning they always seemed to be one step ahead of our security forces."

He added that while the French military effort—quietly aided by several other countries, the United States and Britain included—was efficient, mobile, had lots of armour as well as helicopter gunships, AQIM's biggest ally was the desert. Those vast, desolate stretches of sand and rock that go on forever are his home, his backyard, as it were.

"And it has always been that way, since the beginning of time," declared the French colonel.

At the same time, the machinations of these groups are not always militarily orientated. Recruitment and jihadist indoctrination remains a significant part of the process, as does brutally efficient intimidation, which, in plain language boils down to 'join our ranks or you're dead'.

British journalist Alex West disclosed in what was clearly an intelligence 'leak' that at least one Islamic fundamentalist group had dabbled in biological warfare, as had al-Qaeda in Afghanistan in trying to construct 'Dirty Bombs'. West said there was some evidence that linked AQIM to an outbreak of bubonic plague at one of their training camps in the Algerian outback.[3]

What emerged was that on 19 January 2009 that there had been an outbreak of bubonic plague at an AQIM training camp in Algeria's Tizi Ouzou province and that at least forty jihadists had died from the disease. Surviving AQIM members reportedly fled to other parts of the country hoping to escape infection.

Eli Lake, in an article in *The Washington Times*, made the same claim a day later—based on what he was told by a senior US intelligence official—though he maintained that the incident was not related to bubonic plague. It was an accident involving either a biological or chemical agent, he reported.

In countering this form of terror, France has taken to largely rewriting the counterinsurgency handbook. In effect, the thrust these days is to lead from the front and for this one has to go back a little and look at the rebellion's causative history.

Following a military coup in Bamako on March 2012, something we deal with in a subsequent chapter, al-Qaeda's supreme council quickly moved into the gap calling itself AQIM Coalition Forces. Those units included home-grown Ansar al-Din and MUJAO.

Paris quickly responded and while the Mali engagement was initially intended to be limited to a few thousand troops and aircraft—mainly helicopter gunships and

Mali's interior is vast, troubled and almost undeveloped. Villages like this one are dotted sporadically over an unimaginably massive stretch of Africa.

ground-support jets as well as transport planes, France's military strength in this West African territory by Easter 2013 had peaked to more than 5,000 troops and airmen. It took the French less than a month to drive the rebels from almost all the country's northern cities that included Timbuktu, Kidal and Gao, making the campaign the most successful French military strike since the end of the Algerian War

By now, much of what was happening was taking place more than a thousand kilometres north of Bamako and was headed toward the Adagh des Ifoghas, or Mountains of the Ifoghas tribe, which has been at the core of just about every Tuareg rebellion since the country got its independence from France in 1960.

Shortly before, Kidal, one of the biggest cities in the remote northeast and 1,600 kilometres from Bamako, came into focus. Formerly a Foreign Legion fort, it became the most important forward staging point for counterinsurgency operations after its airport had been seized in an airdrop by French Paras. The battle was intense.

The toughest rebel resistance was encountered in the Adagh, the expansive highlands that stretch well into Algerian territory. Because the terrain is remote and undeveloped and there are no roads to speak of, it became a major obstacle. As one visitor told the BBC, those mountains are a perfect place for a guerrilla army: "The annual rains fill up the gueltas [ponds] with drinking water for nomadic animal herds and insurgents and there are numerous caves that offer shelter from sand storms and helicopter gunships ... The Algerian border is close and porous enough to keep supplies of food, diesel and

French troops preparing for an operation near Timbuktu. The helicopter is the seasoned warhorse, the Aérospatiale Puma.

ammunition flowing in—as long as corrupt local officials can be bribed or forced to turn a blind eye."

More important, it was also from this region that AQIM—in an effort to divert attention from what it intended to do in Mali—launched an attack on an Algerian gas installation at Tigantourine in January 2013. The fact that the target was almost 2,000 kilometres from where AQIM was active in northern Mali signifies both the mobility and extent of influence of this jihadist group. Led by 'Red Beard' Mokhtar Belmokhtar (he dyed his beard with henna), the insurgents made their mark, murdering thirty-nine foreigners and taking 800 hostages. Red Beard managed to escape into the Sahara from there

Before that, in 2004, he was sentenced to life imprisonment in Algeria for forming terrorist groups, robbery, detention and use of illegal weapons. Three years later he was given the death sentence for forming terrorist groups, carrying out armed attacks, kidnapping foreigners, the importing and trafficking of illegal weapons and a year later he was again sentenced to death for murdering thirteen customs officials. In the interim he married four local Berber and Tuareg women from prominent families in northern Mali, cementing his ties in the region. He even named a son Osama after his mentor with whom who he spent time fighting Coalition Forces in Afghanistan.

Belmoktar was at one stage said to have been killed in a remotely operated missile strike involving drones early in 2014, but that turned out to be false, though it did give

an indication that what was then taking place in Mali was starting to resemble the kind of attrition insurgents in Yemen are today facing from distantly launched ordnance. Somehow he seems to have survived numerous onslaughts, though he was reported killed several times in French and Algerian airstrikes.

And alive or dead, the role of Mokhtar Belmokhtar in the Malian uprising is seen as seminal to its military and political outcome. In the broader context, his Algerian terror attack at Tigantourine unquestionably played a role in causing France to review its much-vaunted 'military non-participation status' in West Africa. Almost cast in concrete, those principles were believed by all to be inviolable. Yet, barely a month later the French went into Mali in strength.

One of the anomalies of the ongoing insurgency in Mali is that the Bamako-Senou airport—about fifteen kilometres south of the city—is now one of West Africa's busiest airports with

Rearming a French 'Tigre' gunship.

military flights making up the bulk of it. There are scores of countries either helping France in this ongoing insurgency or busy with retraining and conditioning Mali's armed forces. Countries involved include lightweights like Denmark, Portugal, Morocco, Latvia, Estonia and even Zimbabwe. As a result there is today a constant movement of military aircraft through the country's biggest airport.

On one morning recently, the arrival of a Royal Air Force C-17A Globemaster was followed by a Royal Danish Air Force Hercules C-130, as well as an Antonov 124 'tilt-nose' transporter bringing in more heavy equipment for use in the war. It is notable that many of France's Armée de Terre helicopters were hauled into Mali in the fuselages of these giants in the opening phase of the campaign.

Even South Africa features in the mix. Durban's Starlite Aviation Group mobilized three aircraft to Mali: a Puma 330J, a Bell 407 and a BK-117 helicopter used for medevac purposes, with specialized personnel flying them across Africa to their final destination.

The BK-117 was destined for use by the European Union Training Mission (EUTM) in Mali and followed a circuitous delivery path from Europe. Starlite's chief pilot, the late 'Monster' Wilkins—together with Steve Lodge and Harry Rice—took delivery of the helicopter in Baden Baden and flew it down the West African coast to Mali, a distance of 3,000 nautical miles. Because of the BK's relatively short range, Wilkins intimated afterward that fuel supplies had to be "judiciously managed".

Once in Bamako, the Starlite aviators were surprised at the feverish activity encountered both in the capital and at the airport, underscoring others' observations that Mali's insurgency might have been more serious than the Elysée Palace originally envisaged. But they did discover in Bamako a well-ordered city with skyscrapers going up in

The Lower Sahara is every bit as grim at Iraq's desert regions.

numbers and streets that were cleaner and better kept than any comparable conurbation in their own country.

As former air force brigadier-general Wilkins said, "everybody seemed to be getting into the act" which meant that there was clearly a good level of progress and money to be made. He added that it was not all that surprising since Mali is the continent's fourth largest gold producer with many South African mining houses involved.

When I first approached French Air Force colonel Alain Bayle, France's military attaché in London, with a view to going into Mali to cover the war, he told me that it would be difficult because most of what was taking place was "restricted". But he did confide that his country had deployed almost twenty helicopters to counter this insurrection. If more were needed, he declared, they would follow.

What also became clear was that in spite of being trained by both the United States armed forces (over several years) as well as some European military establishments, Mali's army was not able to withstand AQIM's initial onslaught. Defences in the country's northern cities were in good shape and the army, behind fixed reinforced positions, should have been able to resist. But once on the move, the rebels—in the minds of the defenders—were regarded as formidable.

As a consequence, as soon as it seemed that the defenders of any of the major cities were in the firing line, they abandoned their posts together with much of the armour with which they had been issued—including their weapons and ammunition supplies. The majority needed little encouragement to head south.

For France, the nation that had played a significant role in bringing the Mali national army up to scratch, it was enormously embarrassing, and in the words of one observer, "a complete shambles". It was almost as bad for Washington: the United States military and security personnel had been training Malian military cadres for almost a decade.

According to TomDispatch.com, an outspoken critic of Washington's military efforts abroad (and a project of The Nation Institute), the Americans—who operated under the auspices of its African Command (AFRICOM)—have been involved in all but six or seven African countries in efforts "to rebuild these nations into stable partners with robust, capable militaries". The idea stemmed from creating regional bulwarks that would be favourable to United States' strategic interests in Africa.

Yet, declared TomDispatch, "over the last years, the results have often confounded the planning—with American operations serving as a catalyst for blowback [a term of CIA tradecraft]." The report goes on: "first returns on Washington's new and developing form of 'light footprint' warfare in Africa have hardly been stellar. After [the rebels invaded], Mali went from bulwark to basket case." In turn, this prompted an American-trained army officer—a product of the Pan-Sahel Initiative—to stage a military coup in the Malian capital and oust the democratically elected president of that country. That man was Captain Amadou Sanogo who spoke fluent English and who, for a while, was under arrest in Bamako and claimed by some to have died in custody.

It is necessary to understand conditions under which this war is being fought. In the early 1990s, the nomadic Tuareg of the north began an insurgency over land and cultural rights that persists to this day, despite central government attempts at military and negotiated solutions.

These troubles gathered pace, exacerbated by an enormous influx of high-grade, mostly Eastern Bloc, weapons from the 2011 Libyan civil war, though to be fair, AQIM captured so much military hardware when the Malian army downed tools, they ended up with a surfeit.

The Saharan branch of al-Qaeda was quick to move into an increasingly lawless void. It seized control of the Tuareg regions in the north after the March 2012 military coup, effectively seceding from the rest of Mali and establishing a harsh form of Islamic Sharia law. All forms of music were banned ("ungodly" the Imams declared and not in keeping with Salafist tenets), the destruction of mosques and religious centres in Timbuktu and Gao was commonplace and all female children were banned from schools. The ultra-fundamentalist, Saudi-linked jihadists were in total control; almost a re-enactment of what the Taliban had done in Afghanistan prior to the invasion of that country by Coalition Forces in 2001.

The West African regional grouping Economic Community of West African States (ECOWAS) agreed—with United Nations backing—to launch a coordinated military expedition to recapture the north at a meeting in Nigeria in November 2012, but with preparations expected to take eight or ten months AQIM was not concerned. Obviously, it took a fraction of that time for the Islamists take the initiative and advance toward the government heartland in southwest Mali. Alarmed at the capture of the town of Konna in the north, the Bamako government asked France to intervene militarily.

On the face of it, AQIM had successfully used the most brutal tactics to achieve dominance, but when France, a superior military force, well equipped and well trained, appeared on the scene, it was overwhelmed. That does not suggest they are vanquished: far from it, because it needs only a small number of committed and active jihadists for terror attacks to continue.

Invariably these are suicide attacks and strikes against soft civilian targets like hotels and hospitals and it says a lot that these have since spread to several neighbouring countries.

The first major onslaught launched by the French after the northern cities had been cleared of insurgents was Operation Panthére which took place in the Adagh des Ifoghas mountainous northeast, adjacent to the Algerian frontier.

A difficult enterprise in Lunar-like conditions on the edge of the Sahara, there were more than a thousand troops involved, every man on the ground requiring regular resupply from the air with C-130s dropping pallets by parachute. Vehicle-borne supplies only came later after most of the region was considered reasonably secure and under government control, but only partially because the occasional IED and ambushes still occurred.

Some idea of its extent can be gauged from the fact that ground forces active in this sparse, desert terrain required something like twenty tons of water plus 1,400 combat ration packs every day. When water did occasionally run dry, as sometimes happens in remote backwaters, troops had to resort to sunken wells. But even that was dodgy because of the threat that they had been poisoned.

Having used jets to "treat the target" (as it is euphemistically phrased in Francophonic military parlance) the area was blasted by 250-kilogram bombs delivered by French Air Force Rafales. Roughly 200 al-Qaeda armed militants were killed within days. Troops involved were from 1st Marine Infantry Parachute Regiment, Foreign Legion, as well as

'Tigre' helicopter gunship at Tikmbuktu airport.

Marine Commandos and Air Commandos. These combined elements, which will continue to be used by France in future Sahel operations, often have their own helicopter contingents.

It was never an easy process operating in a tough, baking environment where temperatures easily fluctuated between 40°C in the heat of day to a fraction of that figure after dark.

The average soldier shouldered a sixty-kilogram pack that customarily included six or seven water bottles as well as France's ubiquitous FAMAS assault rifle and enough ammunition to counter an attack. Others marched with the Mini Mitrailleuse (Minimini) machine gun in 5.56mm calibre, a weapon that has proved versatile in a countryside dominated by rocky outcrops and boulders in every direction and which provided good cover for the rebels.

It was in this Ifoghas mountain region that France's helicopter gunship squadrons excelled.

Both the EC-665 four-bladed, twin-engine Tigre and the older Gazelles—supplemented more recently by Eurocopter Cougars—have been useful adjuncts to ground operations, the gunships being advanced versions, fitted with more powerful engines and incorporating high agility and glass cockpits.

Operating in remote parts of the Sahel tends to present its own set of problems, specifically huge volumes of dust being the constant companion of all pilots involved, both on take-off and landing. The problem is partly overcome by air filters which, in turn, need regular attention from ground crews.

French Air Force transport aircraft sent south, together with five Breguet Atlantique 11s that initiated round-the-clock surveillance missions, proved valuable adjuncts to the support effort. Additionally, the air force used Airbus A310s and A340s from 3/60 Estérel Transport squadron for shifting the ground forces.

Washington was also involved in this military struggle—and still is—in Mali and surrounding countries, which explains substantial American drone activity in the conflict. The United States Air Force quickly rose to the occasion, as did the RAF, both with their respective C-17s. France's largest drone base now operates from Niamey in Niger.

Curiously, the arid, rocky terrain of Mali's north favoured both sides. Pilots constantly talked of the inability of spotting rebel groups in remote regions where every rock provides cover. At the same time, the desert terrain makes it almost impossible for AQIM to effect any kind of back-up that involves vehicles, either by day or by night. The moment an unidentified vehicle is spotted it is investigated and here French Air Force Atlantiques come into their own.

It is also one of the reasons why Puma back-up is a constant: very few operations in the north take place without these helicopters—usually operating in tandem—and within radio-hailing distance of ground forces. Pumas also double as gunships, with heavy-calibre machine guns on revolving mounts bolted to the floor just inside the doors. Considering the age of some of these veterans, they seem to have done well.

On paper, the Malian air force should have been able to put more aircraft in the air: fighters, helicopters as well as transports. But almost all its assets date from the Soviet era when Bamako proved to be a strong Cold War stalwart in support of Moscow. Very few of these planes are operational today with almost all fixed wings grounded and only one fully functioning Mi-24. Mali received two Hinds from Bulgaria in 2007, with one lost to enemy action in March 2013.

Some curious stories have emerged as the war progressed. Not long after the French moved in, one of their Special Forces contingents was tasked with capturing an airport in the north where the runway had been blocked by two abandoned armoured vehicles. A reconnaissance flight indicated that there were 900 metres of runway available for a C-130—heavily loaded with troops and equipment as well as armour—to land.

With helicopter gunship top cover, the crew went ahead anyway with an 'assault landing' that involved a squad of the Air Commandos and the Hercules putting down and reversing hard in the final stages. Several MX-10RC light reconnaissance vehicles and troops rolled out and the plane took off again: the entire operation—from touch-down to take-off—took less than three minutes.

It is worth mentioning that shortly before the French went into Mali in force, an American C-130 about to land at a forward operating base with supplies for the local Malian garrison was struck by rebel machine-gun fire. Nobody was injured and the plane made it back to Bamako intact.

Possibly the most hazardous task which French forces have been called upon to do is routine weapons' searches in areas adjacent to where the rebels have been driven off. Though substantial ordnance caches have been uncovered, AQIM tends to bury much of its larger weapons and ammunition without leaving any visible markings as to location: that can result in hefty supplies of enemy hardware left behind to be recovered another day. This is especially prevalent in the mountainous northeast

A surprising development was when French search teams discovered caches of aerial bombs buried in soft sand in remote hideouts that yielded dozens of 12.7mm and 14.5mm anti-aircraft guns. One find revealed five 90kg and a dozen 155kg aerial bombs, all still in their original wooden packing cases. This hardware had originally been looted from Libyan armouries and brought across the Sahara by truck. Once uncovered by French mine-detecting teams, this ordnance was gathered together and buried on the final day and destroyed with an explosive charge laid by engineers to create what is referred to in the vernacular as a *fourneau*, or a furnace.

One of the ironies of the present military campaign in Mali is that this war could have been cut short a few years ago. In February 2012, a sizeable force of South African mercenaries—including some of the same people who were later to tackle Boko Haram in Nigeria—negotiated an $80 million deal with the former president of Mali to counter the rebellion that threatened his government. Apart from a moderate-sized ground force that would tackle the rebels on home turf, the aviation side included two Mi-24 helicopter gunships and four Mi-17 armed support helicopters. The South African private military company (PMC) involved in this venture had originally been offered six Vietnam-era Huey Cobras by an unnamed country at $1 million each, but, according to veteran mercenary aviator Neall Ellis, it was decided to go for Ukrainian Mi-17s instead. The deal for acquiring these aircraft had already been signed and money was about to change hands when Captain Amadou Sanogo, the fairly low-key officer who headed a dissident junta, launched a mutiny that toppled President Amadou Toumani Touré. Referred to be one and all in Mali by his initials ATT, Touré had been in power for a decade and was both bloody-minded and corrupt.

Almost simultaneously, AQIM routed the Malian army and seized the north of the country. Curiously, though military assistance was offered by several African countries, Sanogo rejected all. Initially he was also opposed to French involvement in countering the revolt, but since almost $1 billion was offered in military aid by Western nations to "revitalize the Mali army", the captain—he liked to compare himself with the 'liberator' General de Gaulle—moderated his stance. It says a lot that Captain Amadou Sanogo was among those Malian officers who had been trained by the Americans.

Still, much of what goes on in this remote West African state remains vague. Everybody in the country is aware of the presence of the French military as well as those of their African allies, but little else, especially the extent of casualties these combined forces have inflicted on AQIM. The extensive use of helicopter gunships by the French Air Force almost never features in routine press reports,

Also of interest, is that unlike the original war in Algeria, French losses have been minimal. Casualties among supporting African armies have been much higher, with Chad losing dozens of troops, many in suicide bombings, one of the reasons why security in and around French airbases, while not watertight, is thorough.

The deployment of suicide bombers by rebel commanders is a fairly recent development in this part of Africa and by all accounts, there is no shortage of volunteers. The weapon customarily consists of an explosive belt and is much feared by everybody, soldiers and civilians alike. Unobtrusively worn around the midriff, the belt is of modest thickness and liberally filled with ball bearings together with chunks of steel. There has barely been an operation in Mali where at least one of these belts has not been uncovered by the security forces; their use is widespread.

2. OVERVIEW OF A DESERT CAMPAIGN

There were several reasons why President François Hollande decided to send his armed forces into Mali in January 2013. The collapse of the Malian army, having been trained for years by Western military specialists to counter just such an uprising, was part of it. So was the ability of that force to be able to offer any kind of real military resistance to counter that threat.

Soon after the French reacted militarily to the jihadist invasion of Mali, several observers had to explain exactly what Mali was: not another trouble spot in the Middle East but in Africa and only a few hours' flying time south of Europe. It was also necessary to stress that Mali was threatened by the same brand of Islamic fundamentalists who had caused a civil war in neighbouring Algeria, a conflict that had horrific consequences because it lasted eleven years and resulted in more than 100,000 deaths, probably more.

Essentially, the message was made clear: this new development in the Sahel in 2012 was an issue of enormous importance because the government of Mali could not cope. Nor had it the wherewithal to go it alone militarily or economically, even though it was the fourth biggest producer of gold in Africa. For a start its army was on the run and the Malian air force had barely any serviceable planes.

The Niger is an expansive river and remains a focal point of counter-insurgency operations.

Though the rebels were imposing their own absurd laws and strictures on what had always been an easy-going society that threatened nobody, the implications took some time to emerge. That was when one sage declared that Mali threatened to become a Taliban state on Europe's doorstep.

The long-term implications were even more troubling: "A loose alliance of Islamist movements—two local and one multinational—seeks to turn Mali into the core of a jihadist empire stretching 3,500 kilometres across the notional frontiers of ten states in northern and western Africa from Nigeria to Libya," was the gist of it. The commentator—who may have had government links—went on: "France, the former colonial power, had intervened militarily to prevent the Islamist movements from conquering the south of Mali and despite logistical help from Britain, the United States, Germany and others—coupled to the promise of a pan-West African army getting involved in the future—France had so far acted almost alone."

As might have been expected, this approach had its detractors, some regarding any kind of military action by the French as part of a grand design to recolonize its old African possessions, though clearly that was the last thing that President François Hollande, a committed left-winger and former first secretary of the French Socialist party, even remotely desired.

Nonetheless, options as to how Hollande might tackle matters were few, especially after he had originally been reluctant to intercede after the Tuareg rebellion in Mali's north a year before. Mali, though relatively stable until then, is an enormous country, compared by one knowledgeable wag as a nation that sprawls like a butterfly the size of two Spains across the ethnic and climactic fault-line between Saharan and sub-Saharan Africa.

A starkly beautiful region wracked by war.

The commentator went on to explain that the larger, northern 'wing' of the so-called 'butterfly' consists of desert and semi-desert, inhabited sparsely by Tuareg, Maures and Arabs. The smaller, southern 'wing' is grass, semi-arid scrubland and forest country in the far south and home to roughly 90 percent of almost fifteen million Malians from a variety of different backgrounds.

The decision by Paris to get involved in Mali had not been easy. In part, it was motivated in April 2012 by the Tuareg-orientated Mouvement National pour la Libération de l'Azawad (MNLA) declaring a new Tuareg state. But that was soon overwhelmed by an Islamist breakaway wing and two other Islamist movements. The stronger of these was AQIM, led by a host of foreign fighters including a preponderance of Algerians, which suggested a parallel with the equally diverse French Foreign Legion.

Concurrently, the French defence minister, Jean-Yves Le Drian went on record to declare that his sending French soldiers and aviators to this African military theatre was 'to recapture every square millimetre" of the deserts of northern Mali.

One of the immediate issues facing the French was that they were not dealing with a bunch of novice recalcitrants. Rather, many of the revolutionary cadres involved in the uprising had travelled all the way across the Sahara from Libya, a country where everyday conflict had almost become a way of life. By all accounts, those involved in these hostilities displayed a solid appreciation of military ability.

Worse, the majority of Mali's hardscrabble poor flocked to the appeals of these militant newcomers because they offered both salvation and hope. Their message was clear: the Islamic 'New Order' would help to overthrow a cruel and corrupt government that was propped up by an equally malicious national army.

Also worrying, was that early on, the revolutionaries began to display an uncompromising and often ruthless approach toward those who did not empathize with the ideals of the new Islamic Command. Indeed, many of the recruits that followed the revolutionary call tended to look to the early days of Algeria's upheaval as to what could be achieved. The only real difference between the two countries, some felt, was that in Mali there would be no central government as in Algiers to hold excesses in check.

Tuareg elders at Timbuktu airport to welcome the French military.

So it happened that so-called 'terrorist' groups like Ansar al-Din, al-Tawhid wa al-Jihad and AQIM moved in after the Tuareg Movement for the National Liberation of Azawad had expelled the Malian army from the north and declared a separate country. Almost overnight several radical edicts were imposed, including stoning suspects to death for a variety of 'crimes', tearing down Sufi shrines, and enforcing rigid Sharia law.

Not long afterward the Tuaregs, not at all happy with the kind of uncompromising militancy displayed by the new leadership, were pushed to one side. Many Tuaregs saw no option after being rejected by their putative allies to return to their beloved desert and abandon cities like Timbuktu, Gao, and Kidal to the newfound jihadist groups.

Colonel Haji ag Gamou, the leader of a powerful MNLA brigade, actually defected into neighbouring Niger Republic with all his men after breaking ties with the jihadists. He then returned to southern Mali with his troops to be incorporated into Mali's national army, declaring that he had only acted "to save the lives of my men". He was rewarded for this action by being made a general in the national army and, to be fair, Gamou and his troops have since become a useful ally to the French in their efforts to drive the Islamic radicals out of the north. But some critics were wary, suggesting that having turned once, it was not impossible, if things did not go his way, that Gamou might revert to his old ways.

In a sense, conditions in Mali after the jihadists moved in in early 2012, were very much like the early days of the military revolt in Libya and that implication was not missed by those heading France's ministry of the armed forces at the Hôtel de Brienne in Paris.

Given the militancy of the rebel command, it was impossible not to be aware that these revolutionaries appeared to be intent on plunging the country headlong back into the

Former rebels armed with AK-47s, now fighting with the French in Africa.

Middle Ages. As a result, the sentiment—almost across the board in Paris—was that this was a situation that urgently needed to be checked. In short, somebody had to do something. The word in the French capital began to circulate that the central government in Bamako was on the verge of collapse, underscored in early 2013 that the rebels were only days north of the capital and nobody stood in their way to stop them. There were actually a few similarities with the early days of Taliban fomenting revolution in Afghanistan. Both societies—AQIM and the Taliban—were implacable in their belief, then and still today, that the Shahada, the two-part statement that "there is no god but God; Muhammad is the messenger of God" is absolute, and that it is a fundamental duty of those who follow the teachings of the Qu'ran to destroy those who do not believe.

They were also not all that dissimilar in the way they lived their lives in remote and isolated regions, as they have done for millennia and at a very basic subsistence level. Contemporaneously, they both also share the same ideology as Islamic State whose creed is basic: Non-Muslims have to be subjugated, and in the process either converted or eradicated. In the simplest terms, the revolution in Mali was a furtherance of that dogma.

But sadly, the brutal reality is that in many countries suffering Islamist-orientated upheavals in the modern period—Afghanistan, Syria, Pakistan, Algeria, Egypt after the Arab Spring and elsewhere—an awful lot of both Muslims and Christians had been murdered, because that is how terror is—most times mindlessly indiscriminate.

More serious in the long term, were the jihadists successful in overthrowing the Bamako government, there was every likelihood that like-minded people in several other

Once the French arrived in force, the Tricolor appeared in many public places, almost like magic.

A gunner's-eye view of Timbuktu, an ideal urban guerrilla environment.

West and Central African countries—the Côte d'Ivoire, Burkina Faso, Benin, Chad, Niger, Cameroon, the Central African Republic, Senegal and several more—the majority former French African colonies—might decide to take it upon themselves to do the same. And certainly, once ensconced in Mali, the new Islamic regime would not hold back in offering support, both covert and overt.

As we have all since seen, it did not take long for that threat to become manifest. Terror attacks have taken place in just about all the cities formerly controlled by the French. The Islamic State (Daesh) revolt in Iraq and Syria was clearly waiting in the wings to make things happen and now the same sort of thing was taking place in West Africa.

Far more worrying—for the French especially—was the potential threat toward tens of thousands of French nationals living in these countries, the same people who were working in Africa running businesses, factories, industries, mines, tourist resorts as well as the basic infrastructure of everyday life that would obviously be targeted by a jihadist revolution. Remove all that from the equation of everyday life and a large proportion of Africa's Francophone community—as well as all its markets and commodities—might be lost. More to the point, France (and all of Europe for that matter) was just not ready for an enormous influx of refugees, people of all races, each one of them desperate to avoid the kind of fundamentalism being offered by AQIM. This was the reason why so many European countries rallied to Hollande's call for military help when it came.

Prior to France taking action, the kind of news reports coming out of West Africa after AQIM began to flex its muscles resulted in Washington issuing a series of warnings about travel in this part of Africa. One of these, dated July 26, 2011, read as follows: "The Department of State continues to warn U.S. citizens of the risk of travel to Mali, and to recommend against all travel to the north of the country due to kidnapping threats against Westerners. As noted in the Department of State's Worldwide Caution dated July 26, 2011, al-Qaida in the Maghreb (AQIM) has declared its intention to attack Western targets. The Department is aware of several separate sources of information indicating AQIM's ongoing interest in kidnapping Westerners throughout the Sahel region. Joint Mali–Mauritania military operations against AQIM in July–August 2011 have also increased the risk of terrorist retaliation in northern Mali. The U.S. Embassy in Bamako has issued several emergency messages for U.S. citizens regarding these threats, as have the U.S. Embassies in Ouagadougou, Burkina Faso, Nouakchott, Mauritania and Niamey, Niger."

On January 5, 2011, an individual claiming connections to AQIM attacked the French embassy in Bamako with a handgun and an improvised explosive device. Two injuries were reported. On January 7, 2011, two French nationals were kidnapped in Niamey, Niger. They were found dead less than twenty-four hours later following a rescue attempt by French and Nigerien military forces. On February 2, 2011, a vehicle containing explosive materials failed to stop at a security checkpoint outside of Nouakchott, Mauritania.

Mauritanian security forces opened fire and the vehicle exploded, killing the vehicle's passengers. Mauritanian security forces were on alert for suspected AQIM vehicles that possibly had entered Mauritania to conduct terrorist attacks. In early February 2011, an Italian woman was kidnapped in southern Algeria, and it is likely that she was held for a while in northern Niger or Mali.

The region has seen an increase in insurgent-led violence in recent years. Five French nationals, a Togolese national, and a Malagasy national were kidnapped from the uranium-mining town of Arlit, Niger in September 2010, four of whom are still held hostage by AQIM. One hostage, a French national, was executed by the rebel group in retaliation for the killing of six AQIM militants during a French-led Mauritanian-launched rescue operation in Mali's north.

The authorities in both Bamako and N'Djamena warn that because of France's determination to counter

A side-gunner's-eye-view of an area along the Niger river where rebels have been active.

these atrocities, more such retaliatory attacks are likely in the future and would include other Western 'targets of opportunity'.

As one local authority from the Niger Republic stated: "In addition to threats posed by AQIM and potential hostage takers, violent confrontations between rival drug and arms traffickers have occurred in northern Mali over the past year. The threat posed by AQIM, sporadic banditry, and the porous nature of Mali's northern borders with Algeria, Niger, and Mauritania all reinforce longstanding security concerns affecting travel to northern Mali."

It came as a shock then when I was made aware that a close associate in the United States with whom I regularly exchanged messages had come within a whisker of being taken hostage by an al-Qaeda group that had already murdered some of their victims. That happened in November 2011, when Brian Gaisford, owner of Hemingways—New York's most prominent African art gallery at the Manhattan Art and Antiques Centre on Second Avenue—took a group of his clients into a remote part of West Africa 'spotting' for the elusive Malian desert elephant.

He'd bounced the idea off me a short while before and even suggested that I come along. Pressure of work and an uneasy feeling about what was going on just then in West Africa obliged me to decline, though I would dearly have loved to visit some of the old haunts again, Bamako the capital city especially. I might then even have considered taking the train back to Dakar in Senegal once the safari was over and possibly get in a bit of diving off Goreé Island, the old slaving fort that has become popular with visitors in recent years.

Soldiers and civilians meet for conflab at Gao. (Photo ICRC)

I had reservations of course and I said so: al-Qaeda in the Maghreb, backed by Tuareg dissidents, I told him, had become active in the region, ominously so. The Malian army had launched a series of operations against armed jihadis operating along the Niger river. There had been casualties and deaths on both sides. I voiced my fears in an email, saying that tourist groups going into the desert out of Bamako were few and far between, adding that he would almost certainly "be monitored by some of the people you encounter along the way and possibly come to harm, so think carefully about this venture".

Brian replied the same day, maintaining that arrangements were too far advanced and that they were going ahead anyway.

"OK, I hear what you say," were his words. "I am off to Mali on 27 October with a group of seven and we'll back in the US on 9 November. Keith Joubert will be with us as well ... he will be doing some work on the desert elephant." Keith Joubert was a wildlife artist that I knew only by reputation, having always admired his work but unable to afford them; I was aware too that he often travelled to remote African destinations with Brian Gaisford.

I then contacted another old friend and co-author Jerry Conley in Washington and asked for his opinion about the trip since there had been other reports of problems in some of the more remote regions in the African Sahel. Jerry's immediate reaction was that to go into the interior of Mali at that time—especially the north, around Timbuktu— would not be clever. He even attached the above State Department travel warning, compiled by the Bureau of Consular Affairs and issued to prospective visitors to Mali.

Timbuktu by then had been especially badly affected by the jihadists. Founded by Tuareg tribes between the fifth and twelfth centuries, the city has been nicknamed 'The City of 333 Saints', referring to the number of Muslim sages buried there. During a halcyon period in the fifteenth and sixteenth centuries, the city was revered as a great centre of Islamic learning—but for the fanatics who arrived more recently, its moderate form of Islam was idolatrous.

I passed all that information onto my friend in New York but it made no difference. I countered by warning him that the moment his tiny convoy left the comparative safety of Bamako, he would be on his own. Furthermore, AQIM was very well organized, was acutely versed in operational intelligence, which included the activities of 'infidels' like himself and his party. They would unquestionably have somebody observing their actions, I suggested.

His only comment to that remonstration was that his daughter, Logan, would be manning the safari desk in the office and "she will contact you if I get into any crap in Northern Mali. Whatever you do, don't pay any ransom ... I'm not worth it." As it happened, Brian Gaisford and his party returned safely to New York a few weeks later. As he told me on the phone, "we had a really great trip."

But then, little more than a week later, in roughly the same area that he and his friends had visited—and from the same hotel where they had stayed for several days—another tour group was attacked and one of their members murdered. That followed the abduction of what AQIM operatives declared were two "French spies" as well as three other Europeans in Mali only days before. In a statement sent to Agence France-Presse in Rabat, a spokesman for al-Qaeda in the Islamic Maghreb said it was responsible for the November 24, 2012 kidnapping of a pair of French nationals and three other Europeans in Timbuktu:

"We will soon make our demands known to France and Mali," it declared. The two French nationals were Philippe Verdon and Serge Lazarevic who, the al-Qaeda statement claimed, "work for the French intelligence services." They were seized at gunpoint from their hotel in the town of Hombori near the border with Niger. What the report did not say was that the hotel at Hombori was where Brian Gaisford and his party had overnighted.

Then something even more disturbing arrived. Datelined Bamako, Mali, November 16, 2012, an Associated Press report headed "German killed; Dutch, South African, Swede seized" read as follows: "Gunmen killed a German man in Mali's most famous city of Timbuktu and seized three men from the Netherlands, South Africa and Sweden, their tour guide said, as officials on Saturday ordered a plane to evacuate foreigners from the tourist destination. Tour guide Ali Maiga said the South African man also holds a British passport. Maiga was with the tourists during Friday's attack at a Timbuktu restaurant. A witness and an official said gunmen burst into the restaurant, grabbed four tourists dining there and executed one of them when he refused to climb into their truck."[1]

The report went on to explain that until a few years ago, Timbuktu had been one of the most visited destinations in Africa, "but it is now one of the many former tourist hotspots in Mali that have been deemed too dangerous to visit by foreign embassies because of kidnappings".

It also reported that the abductions had yet to be claimed by AQIM "whose members have kidnapped and ransomed more than fifty Europeans and Canadians since 2003. If Friday's kidnapping is by AQIM, it will mark the first time they have taken a hostage inside of Timbuktu's city limits.

"Thursday's event would be another first—the first hostage taking south of the Niger river. The group's footprint has grown dramatically since 2006, when the Algerian-led cell first joined al-Qaeda. Security experts estimate the group has been able to raise around $130 million from ransom payments alone."

Brian Gaisford's response to all this was interesting. His email a few days later was explicit, accompanied by half a dozen photographs of where the drama had unfolded. Referring to the attachments, he said: "This is the small hotel in Hombori where we stayed and from where the two were just kidnapped. Everyone just sleeps on the roof although the rooms have VERY strong doors and bars across all the windows. The rooms were almost like cells, so we all just slept out in the open.

"When we tracked the elephant, we just lay out in the open with the Tuareg all around us ... there was no security in Mali ... no roadblocks at all. I am sure that would help. I am going back there in January. Come with me."

Some days later Gaisford communicated once more and added a postscript: "A week later and I could have been with these so-called spies. They took the cell phones from the hotel owner and the cook in Hombori and those two have since been released. Ibrahim, our tracker as well, I think. I'm convinced that he was an [al-Qaeda] informant but he seemed to like our group, probably because we're big tippers. He was not from the area and looked more like a Somali ... How hard would it have been for the Mali Army to have tracked them in the desert? There was no wind or rain to wipe the tracks of the people responsible. Especially in the soft desert-like sand north of Timbuktu ... With even a single [helicopter] they could have got them chop-chop." I answered later that same day, "You are very lucky man, Brian."

3. FRANCE'S FIFTY-YEAR CONQUEST OF THE SAHEL

More than 150 years before Operation Serval evolved into Operation Barkhane, a much earlier generation of soldiers fought long and hard to subjugate vast tracts of sub-Saharan Africa that stretched from Senegal almost to the Nile. That war lasted fifty years, and while not everybody in present-day France readily recalls that period of their country's colonial history, the majority of West Africans will tell you today that they find it difficult to forget.

Strictly speaking—though some French old timers would argue otherwise—it was a tough, long-winded war of imperial conquest and followed hard on the heels of what had already been going on militarily in Algeria since the early 1800s.

The French conquest of Algeria took place between 1830 and 1847, sparked in 1827 by a minor spat between the ruler of the Ottoman Regency of Algiers and the French consul. It soon escalated into a naval blockade, after which France invaded and seized Algiers. Thereafter French forces rapidly took control of all the other coastal communities. Once in command of Algeria's most fertile regions, Paris vigorously encouraged the immigration of large numbers of French nationals to Algeria in part, it was claimed, to "bring good civilization to our new Arab subjects".

For the French military, the seventeen-year Algerian campaign that followed—much of it in isolated mountain and desert-like terrain well south of the Mediterranean—provided future generations of French soldiers with the kind of learning curve they would need for the expansion of a vast colonial empire, not only in Africa but across the globe.

It was axiomatic perhaps, that having dispatched Algeria's so-called 'Old Order', Paris would start looking for more opportunities of expanding its colonial fife. The African continent, close to Europe and with much of its interior still unexplored, offered the best prospects.

The switch to conquests that lay farther south started from the French naval base at the mouth of the Senegal river. Originally founded by Marseilles commercial interests in the seventeenth century, European merchants had chosen St Louis—a two- or three-day camel ride north of the still tiny settlement at Dakar—as their headquarters.

Trade—including that of slaves—must have been good because Paris instructed its garrison commander to construct a fort on an island off St Louis, which would consolidate its pre-eminence along this stretch of coast: the port became a French naval base after the defeat of Napoleon.

Everything linked to colonial conquest was notched up several gears with the arrival of General Louis Faidherbe, France's arch empire-builder. Once ensconced in Dakar he created an army of Senegalese troops that became the basis of the extension of French military power in West Africa. Ruthlessly ambitious and with a relatively free hand, he embarked on a series of military campaigns that brought many of the coastal regions farther south under his control. He then chose to strike inland toward present-day Mali

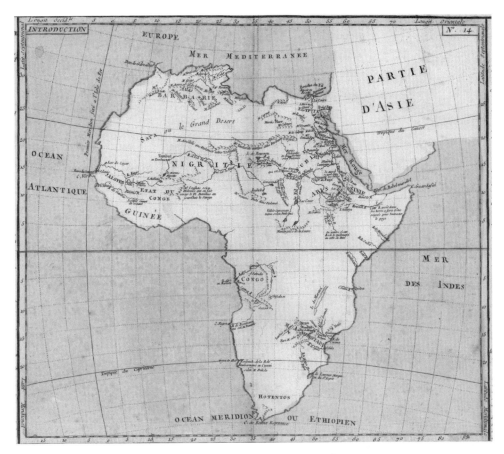

This 1787 French map shows how little was known of the West African interior.

and beyond. There were dozens of campaigns into the 'Dark Interior' as some referred to that part of Africa, not all of them successful. But then the Europeans had guns and the natives did not. Also, even with Napoleon out of the way, France by then was an accomplished military power and easily able to bamboozle locals with sophisticated tactics.

It did not take long for this European presence to be challenged by a host of traditional African leaders who deeply resented the intrusion of the white man into their territories, building forts and claiming disputative rights and, as might have been expected, these black leaders reacted accordingly. Trading for gold or slaves or palm wine was fine, but to claim swathes of African territory as a future colony was not.

As the British writer P. C. Wren manages to impart in his marvellous *Beau Geste* adventure books about the wars the French Foreign Legion fought in Africa, nothing was easy. The Africans were all but immune to many of the tropical diseases that cut down European campaigners, sometimes within days of their arrival in the tropics, though things got better once they moved into the semi-desert interior. Also, black fighters were familiar with the terrain and its secrets and in this respect the French were comparative novices.

An 1858 depiction of Timbuktu.

Some of the African leaders like Umar El Hadj, a Muslim cleric from Timbuktu whose domain stretched southward all the way to the Niger river, fought several campaigns against the European invaders, until he and his son were killed in action in 1864. His illustrious life and many victories are still celebrated in that ancient city today.

Samory Touré was another recalcitrant guerrilla fighter who displayed brilliant and innovative efforts that used ambush and surprise to thwart the French. He operated farther west and built up an empire that stretched almost from the coast to the old trading city on the Niger river, Mopti. Touré kept Paris on the hop for decades, until he was captured in 1898 and exiled—with four of his wives—to an island off the coast of present-day Gabon.

The French/British writer Sanche de Gramont gives an excellent account of what was taking place in both the French and British spheres of interest in West Africa in his historical book on the Niger river *The Strong Brown God*: "the conquest of the upper Niger was entirely due to ambitious field commanders testing their theories of pre-emptive attack, and the conquest of the lower Niger was due to English explorers, traders and abolitionists. In both cases the respective governments were dragged in to regulate a de facto situation of conquest. The French officer turned colonial expansion into an epic while the English turned it into a balance sheet. On the lower Niger the Union Jack followed commerce and on the upper Niger the Tricolor fluttered at the head of military columns."

The other issue, as de Gramont relates, was the half-century war of conquest that the French fought from the mid-1800s onward against the standing armies of two powerful

French colonial troops and Legionnaires arriving in Dahomey preparatory to moving north toward the Niger river, 1892.

African empires. "They laid siege to and captured the principal river cities and each year during the dry season there was a four-month military campaign against African leaders who fought to maintain their territorial independence from European intruders."

Also a reality was that while the British tended to leave control of native regions to their traditional leaders or *sardaunas* (sultans) in what became known as 'Indirect Rule', the French overwhelmed tribal leaders and attempted to govern their African possessions in the same way that they governed Brittany or the Auvergne. And while critics argue that the French model resulted in acculturation, other historians contend that the French way generated integration. All acknowledge that the end result was the same: domination.

In a sense, the French believed that they were a race like the ancient Greeks, with the gift for transmitting the highest forms of civilization. They wished to create their parts of Africa in their own image, as it were. At its core was the naïve belief that every African tribesman under their control was a Frenchman. Obviously, the majority of African people did not agree. While most African people living under the French flag accepted their rule, regarding it as a kind of institutionalized 'protection' against warrior tribes in the interior, most of their black leaders despised the French. They only agreed to work with what Paris had to offer after their regions had been subdued and then, more often than not, to save their skins.

In the early 1880s, a French officer, Lieutenant-Colonel Borgnis-Desbordes, an admirer of the American 'go-ahead' principle, took twenty officers and about 400 men and set out on a punitive expedition to destroy the villages of a chief who had refused to subject his people to French rule. Using ground forces, cannon and gunboats on the river, he wielded a heavy stick to keep the locals under control.

In 1883, his forces now firmly established on the Niger, Borgnis-Desbordes received a letter (in a cleft stick) from one of the local chiefs who regarded the French with particular disdain. For Africa at the time, it was a fairly lengthy diatribe and it read: "To the uncircumcised son of the uncircumcised, colonel Desbordes, may God confound and

COMBAT DE DOGBA, 19 SEPTEMBRE 1892.

French colonial troops repelling an atack at Dogba, in present-day Benin.

cause you to perish with your partisans because none is so great an evildoer and traitor as you are. You say you only wish to make a commercial route. That is false and contrary to good sense and reason. Your desire is to destroy the country, close the roads and make war on the Believers."

For all of France's early military successes in Algeria and other parts, there was never enough manpower to control so vast a west and central African region. This was an enormous part of Africa subsequently subdivided into more than twenty-five countries and during the colonial epoch, ruled by France, Britain, Germany, Spain, Portugal and Italy, with Paris grabbing the biggest chunks.

As an indirect consequence the Légion Étrangère or French Foreign Legion came into being, employed to protect and expand France's colonial empire for much of the nineteenth century. Initially stationed only in Algeria, Foreign Legion operations were soon expanded to include much of Equatorial Africa to the south, its numbers drawn from among thousands of seasoned veterans who had fought in European campaigns that had plagued Europe since the Napoleonic wars.

General Faidherbe made an effort to enhance his influence still further by the creation in 1857 of a native infantry corps. Here again the colonialist bugbear surfaced. It had nothing to do with goodwill toward Africans, but rather a means to conquer more of their territory. One of Faidherbe's quotes about conditions in Senegal at the time bears testimony: "other colonies give us products ... this one gives us manpower."

Foreign Legion troops in the northern Saharan region, 1914. The original caption states that this is Captain Leclerc's company drawing rations.

Working in tandem with Paris's newly created African army, the Régiment Étranger—by now a home for foreign adventurers, social misfits, and every kind of criminal—soon became the military workhorse of French colonialism. Adopting the motto *Legio patria nostra*—the Legion is our fatherland—in the 1840s, it made its headquarters in Sidi-bel-Abbès in Algeria and went on to play a significant role in the French conquest of that country as well.

But Faidherbe was also making demands in his thrusts into the interior from present-day Senegal and from early on Foreign Legion elements were sent to Senegal to serve under his command.

Explorers had made known the riches and possibilities of the region along the length of the Niger and Faidherbe was determined to add those territories to France's dominions. He even dreamed of creating a French African empire stretching from Senegal to the Red Sea. In the process he obliged weaker states to sign protectorates and, when he considered the time appropriate, went to war with the Toucouleur empire along the Niger and the Cayor farther south.

While most of these obscure place names and phrases are hardly likely to enthuse the average reader, it is important to accept that what Faidherbe was doing at the time inspired several other countries to get in on the act. Soon Britain, Germany and Portugal were drawing lines across maps, often in total disregard of claims made by several other countries. These issues were only finally thrashed out at the Berlin Conference of 1884–5 when all the states with colonial interests in Africa sat down and attempted to establish what areas belonged to whom.

By the time that Faidherbe finally left West Africa in 1865, he had achieved what few of his successors were able to accomplish in later years. From a remote outpost near the frontier with what was later to become Mauretania, he established the Bank of Senegal, published a newspaper and taught the locals how to grow groundnuts for export to France through what was to become the biggest entrepôt between Tangiers and Cape Town. He also created an exclusive school for the sons of native chiefs and notables so that they could get what he termed "a proper French education".

Additionally he raided his modest treasury and established a school for translators so that local functionaries and his own people could properly communicate, in French, of course.

A rail link into the interior linking Dakar with Bamako followed in later years, without which the pace of development would have stultified. As with the British in Africa, communications were a priority and such efforts certainly helped change the nature of the entire continent from a hopeless, disorganized amalgam of tribes and cultures into one of fairly reliable cohesion.

There were some unexpected developments, good and bad. In July 1857, Faidherbe formed a new military unit of native infantry, the Tirailleurs Sénégalais. African troops were signed up for two years and paid fifty centimes a day, plus uniform and a regular job. As Sanche de Gramont comments, "to naked natives pounding grain in the primitive bush, all this seemed rather magnificent, and there were so many re-enlistments that the Tirailleurs soon acquired the polish and discipline of a professional corps of colonial infantry in the French Army and went on to see active service through two world wars."

Legionnaires march past their colours in this typically 'Beau Geste'-type Saharan fort, mid-1950s.

By then they were active and recruited in all of France's African possessions and in World War I the Tirailleurs provided around 200,000 troops, more than 135,000 of whom fought in Europe. Roughly 30,000 of their number were killed in action.

Of note here is that the Tirailleurs fought for the French in Algeria and the last Senegalese unit in the French Army was disbanded in 1964. It is also worth mentioning that the last Senegalese *tirailleur* to have served in the Great War was Abdoulaye Ndiaye who died at the age of 104 in November 1998. He had been wounded in the Dardanelles.

With Faidherbe gone, others took his place, the centre of control gradually moving south, first to Goree Island and then Dakar. France's takeover of vast regions in the interior continued apace.

In 1883, French Army captain J. S. Gallieni occupied Bamako on the banks of the Niger river, then a sprawling conurbation and a major regional African trading centre that owed much of its prestige to the ancient Islamic city and gold trading centre of Timbuktu, a thousand kilometres to the north.

In the quest of acquiring new lands, especially in Africa, France established a number of military units. The first was Armée d'Afrique (African Army) created in June 1830 to "conquer, occupy and pacify" various parts of the continent, starting in North Africa and, over many decades, gradually working their way south. Zouave units followed, then the African Hunters in 1831, Algerian Sharpshooters ten years later and the corps of the Spahis in 1843. The Zouaves were French units of light infantry attached to the African Army and their recruitment, until World War II, was exclusively European.

4. THE FRENCH FOREIGN LEGION

"Everybody wants to be a Legionnaire until it's time to be a Legionnaire. Shake hands with COMLE [Commandement de la Légion Étrangère] as he gives you your *Certificate de Service Militaires* and only then can you start talking about actually being a Legionnaire."

Blog on the Legion's website

I have only been to war once with anybody who had served in the French Foreign Legion and that was Phil Foley, who, in the public domain preferred to use his nom de guerre Paul Fanshaw. Paul, as the Yanks like to say, was "one tough fella". Tough, lean and mean as hell, he was incredibly fit. In his U.S. Army days (he served in Special Forces in Vietnam) he played wide receiver on an army team when military football was the equivalent of semi-pro smash mouth football. In the Legion he made their top cross-country team and even later, in El Salvador, where I met him on operations, he could easily outpace us all, including the nineteen- or twenty-year-old government army conscripts, many of whom were on home turf in those hills. Paul was in Tahiti when he deserted the Legion in a hurry, having apparently been exposed as an agent of the U.S Government. All he would say was "French intelligence was after me" and offer no explanation. Not even how he got off the

The Legion in action.

islands and back to the States. There was some talk of CIA involvement because being a French possession it would have been impossible for him to have left the islands legally.

Having made *sergeant chef* he would have drawn $2,500 a month in retirement had he voluntarily gone back to France and served the mandatory six months for deserting, but he stayed put once he got back Stateside. Furthermore, the Legion counted one day toward retirement for every static line jump; two days for each free fall. Phil had 284 jumps, which would have brought him to retirement age. I once asked him why he didn't turn himself in so he could retire. No answer.

Phil Foley died in his bed a few years ago and his mién was typical of those who served in that distinguished unit, which for almost two centuries has prided itself on being the *corps d'elite* of the French army, though the Legion itself often disdains that association. Which raises the question: why did so many young men join those ranks in the old days when about all that could be offered newcomers was an exceptional *esprit de corps*. The dismal pay scale certainly belied the traditional jibe that legionnaires were simply mercenaries. These days, prospective recruits are thoroughly vetted—and that includes INTERPOL—before being put through their paces. But previously, for reasons possibly best kept to themselves, the assurance of anonymity, a fresh start in life, a sense of purpose, and good potential for advancement were attractive inducements for enlistment and service, though only French nationals could make commissioned rank. Most important for so many, was the prospect of unbridled excitement offered by the Legion, though the possibility of perishing in the process went unsaid.

On parade.

Legionnaires who served in Africa in the 1800s—mostly in the Sahara Desert or regions farther south—were a lot better off than being sent to Mexico, Spain or Crimea as enemy weaponry in Africa tended to be the occasional flintlock. Through it all you always went on foot; only officers had camels or horses.

Nonetheless, while stories of French Foreign Legion exploits did the rounds and highlighted small and lonely group actions from remote forts, the loss of life was prodigious. The number of legionnaires killed on active service, all told, is said to number about 40,000.

Nowadays, the Legion is an ultra-elite unit that includes Special Forces, Airborne, engineering, armoured cavalry and a host of other demanding disciplines. It continues to serve in Chad, Mali, the Côte d'Ivoire and elsewhere in the Atlantic, Pacific and Indian oceans.

Indeed, the days of a man escaping his past in the Legion are as long vanished as marauding Berber tribes and as one writer picturesquely described it not so long ago, "Forts at the edge of the world".

Among the first French deployments in Mali to go into action once the decision had been made to tackle AQIM at source was the Legion. Two weeks after the first French troops went into action in Mali, backed by jet fighter aircraft and helicopter gunships, 200 legionnaires of the 2nd Foreign Parachute Regiment (2e REP) were dropped immediately north of Timbuktu by parachute. Once an ancient trading city, it had become the key to Islamic revolution in the north.

They were joined by French soldiers backed by armour from several other French units, including legionnaires from 1er REC and it did not take the combined force long to drive the rebels out of all of Mali's northern cities and towns.

Legion engineers repairing a bridge, Mali.

From there the men of 2e REP moved into the Adrar mountains in the northeast where they spent a month patrolling and searching for hideouts among high points and rocks. By all accounts there were many and firefights were regular. In the end, with some of their leaders killed, the survivors fled into Algeria.

Operation Netero and Operation Météorite followed in early August 2013 with three companies of legionnaires (together with troops from Mali and the Republic of Niger) searching for rebels and arms caches to the east and southeast of Gao in a huge quadrant roughly a hundred kilometres square.

One of the unusual Foreign Legion units is its Surveillance & Direct Action Platoon (Section de renseignement et d'intervention offensive, or SRIO) of the 2nd Engineer Regiment of the Foreign Legion, whose sappers weeks later participated in a series of road-clearing operations for regular French army convoys

Altogether, more than 450 airborne-rated legionnaires attached to 2e REP took part in these military operations and so it went on for the rest of the year, with similar patterns constantly emerging. Six months later the 2nd Foreign Parachute Regiment, the only airborne unit of the Legion, became active elsewhere in West Africa.

April, 2015 brought another development with Legion parachute contingents making jumps in the vicinity of the Salvador Pass of northern Niger, on the border with both Libya and Algeria. This region, as the French term it, is "Deep Saharan Territory", and for the insurgents the pass was, and is, an important crossroads for the drug and arms trafficking carried out by radical Islamist groups and local rebel and criminal gangs.

Legionnaires on desert operations.

From Mali in 2015, other units headed into Chad and Niger, all part of Operation Barkhane, successor to Operation Serval.

The 1st Company 2nd Foreign Parachute Regiment was based in Madama, a new French forward operating base located in what locals referred to as 'The Land of Nowhere' located in the remotest northeastern corner of Niger, near the Libyan–Algerian border. Work there involved searches for drug and arms and the arrest of suspects in a vast area that abuts the Sahara.

Midyear 2015 saw 300 troops from France, Niger and Chad involved in Operation Aghrab in southeastern Niger along the border with Chad. At the same time, the Legion tested its operational ability in desert warfare. It is notable that French Foreign Legion operations are concurrent in numerous regions across the world. In June 2013, as we have seen, their troops were active on a large scale in Mali, Chad, the Niger Republic, with elements from the 2nd Foreign Parachute Regiment (2e REP) and an instruction team in Senegal. In the Côte d'Ivoire there was the 1st Foreign Cavalry Regiment (1er REC) and a squadron from the 1st Foreign Engineer Regiment (1er REG). Farther afield at the same time there was minesweeping/demining element working the terrain, and, detached from the 1st Foreign Engineer Regiment (1er REG), a platoon from the same regiment in the United Arab Emirates as well as a company from 2e REI.

On the Indian Ocean island of Mayotte (Comoros), the Foreign Legion has an instructional unit, as well as further elements in Reunion, French Guyana, Tahiti and elsewhere.

The Legion's Fort de Nogent, on the Marne, near Paris.

French commandos and Legionnaires of GCP 2ème REP on operations in the desert.

It all goes back a long time. In 2016, the French Foreign Legion's 2nd Foreign Infantry Regiment (2e REI) commemorated the 175th anniversary of its activation. Though it all started in Algeria, the Legion has fought in Algeria, Crimea, Italy, Mexico, French Indochina, Madagascar, Morocco, France, Chad, Iraq, Yugoslavia, Côte d'Ivoire, Mali and in the Central African Republic. Currently 2e REI is also the largest regiment of the Foreign Legion.

For those interested, it boils down to this: during selection you will be told that your first engagement is for five years. You will be carefully made aware of the restrictions that will be forced upon you while serving in the region during your stay in Aubagne in France (where you are initially put through our paces). Several times you will be pointedly asked whether you are certain that you wish to spend the next half-decade of your life as a legionnaire. If not, you have the option to leave, there and then. If you make it to Castel (Castelnaudary), the training base in Aude near Toulouse in the south, you will have answered yes every time you are asked.

In a review of two books on the Legion by military historian Max Hastings in the October 14, 2010 edition of the *New York Review of Books*, headed "The Hard Truth About the Foreign Legion", he makes some interesting observations: "The world contains more misfits, sadists, masochists, and people who enjoy fighting than we sometimes like to suppose. How else can one explain the fact that the French Foreign Legion is heavily over-recruited? In an age when most of the world's armies strive to make military service a less

A Foreign Legion base near Timbuktu.

bestial and more enlightened experience than it used to be, the Legion still drives its trainees to scrub floors manically, fold kit and uniforms with obsessive precision, and march, march, march.

"Nothing much about its culture has changed since the German recruit Erwin Rosen, quoted by Adrian Gilbert in *Voices of the Foreign Legion*, wrote in the early 1900s: 'It is always being drummed into the legionnaire that he is intended for nothing else in this world except for marching. If the pangs of hunger are gnawing at his stomach or thirst parches his tongue, that is so much the worse for him, but it is no reason for his not marching on! He may be tired, dead tired, completely exhausted—but he must not stop marching. If his feet are bleeding and the soles burn like fire, that is very sad—but the marching pace must not be slackened. The sun may burn till his senses are all awhirl, he must go on.'"

About those who have seen the legionnaires march impressively on parade, perhaps down the Champs-Élysées on Bastille Day with their controlled long step, Hastings knowingly quips, "[you] may not realize what lies behind it."

He quotes something written in 1924 by an Englishman J. Woodhall Marshall, one of 40,000 foreign volunteers who sought to aid France in her hour of peril and were drafted into the regiment when he wrote home: "The Legion is the strangest thing ever thought up in the mind of man. In my room ... there is myself, an Irishman; and my next neighbour is an American; and the other inhabitants include an ex-officer of a South American Republic, who came specially over ... for the war, and is my greatest friend, a Dutch solicitor, a Russian Jew, three Cossacks, two Italians, a student from a Russian university, an Englishman who has always been resident in Paris and can hardly speak English, a Spaniard, and other mysterious individuals whose identity is absolutely hid."

Some famous people have passed through the Legion's ranks in the almost two centuries that it has been active. These include HRH Prince Aage of Denmark, Crown Prince Bảo Long of Vietnam, head of the Nguyễn Dynasty (the deposed Emperors of Vietnam), HSH Prince Louis II of Monaco, as well as Peter I, King of Serbia.

Hastings makes the point that the British author P. C. Wren was responsible for wrecking the domestic felicity of several upper-class European families by writing his 1924 novel *Beau Geste*, which persuaded some troubled adolescents that a romantic destiny awaited them amid desert sands. This is surprising since it has always been accepted that throughout its history, the Legion and the fighters who make up its ranks were seen as expendable. Foreigners continue to join, accepting the possibility of death in a far-off place in exchange for a new life with some sense of purpose.

Curious stories have emerged, almost all, if not rational, are usually based on events that actually took plane. Like the episode in Wren's book of the fallen soldiers, killed while defending the fort, being propped up by Sergeant-Major Lejaune to create the impression that they were still alive. Faced with insuperable odds, Lejaune had an idea: "as each man fell, we lifted him and propped him up behind with a bayonet and stood him against the parapet. When the sergeant went out we stuck his pipe in his mouth and he looked regular life-like, only more determined. Soon there was a row of dead men guarding the blockhouse, and they looked so calm and confident that the Oulad-Seghir [attacking rebels] evidently thought it would be too risky to come to close quarters with us ... and gave up their attempt on the post in disgust, so that when some of our men [from another unit] came to our rescue at the double there was nothing for them to do."

Head of the French Army, General Bertrand Ract-Madoux salutes the colours of 2ème REI at Gao, Mali.

Legionnaires and Malian troops conducting search operations.

A French column on the move.

La Légion étrangère.

Which brings us back to the modern period and my American friend who deserted from the Legion because he was caught spying for the CIA, Sergeant Chef Phil Foley. Phil was in the first contingent of legionnaires dropped into the Congolese mining town of Kolwezi on May 17, 1978. The unit was only extracted eight days later and Operation Leopard (Operation Bonite in France) has gone down as one of the toughest scraps in which the French Foreign Legion was involved since the battle of Dien Bien Phu.

Essentially, it involved the rescue of more than 2,000 Europeans, mostly miners and their families who had been taken hostage by a group of Katangese from the rebel Congolese National Liberation Front and who called themselves 'Tigers'.

Trouble started on May 13 when roughly 1,500 Katangese rebels invaded the city of Kolwezi and grabbed as hostages just about every European they encountered, most of them of French or Belgian origin. Drunk or drugged, they went berserk and started looting. Still not satisfied, the fighters, by now totally out of control went on to murder local residents as well as some of the Europeans in their custody.

The government in Kinshasa asked Belgium, France, Morocco and the United States to restore order. Paris told the Legion to prepare for action and it was mostly American aircraft that took them in. Foley was at the forefront of that effort, attached to the 2nd Foreign Parachute Regiment (2e REP) and, as he explained, they had their work cut out because the enemy, even half-sober, was tough, experienced and well trained. Also, they had all the weapons they needed, having driven off the local gendarmerie and raided their arsenals.

The official number of dead rebels, Phil told me, was put out as being in the hundreds. In truth, he said, he and his men probably ended up killing more than a thousand. The final official tally was more than 2,100 Europeans rescued, about 160 Europeans and 600 locals massacred by rebels, 247 rebels killed, 163 captured, five legionnaires killed and twenty-five legionnaires wounded.

5. THE TUAREGS AND AQIM

"According to the Greek historian Herodotus, the Tuaregs are a people who were living in northern Mali at about the time he was alive, almost 2,500 years ago. Later reports suggest that after establishing the city of Timbuktu in the eleventh century, these people 'traded, travelled, and conquered throughout the Sahara' over the next four centuries, eventually converting to Islam 700 years ago, 'which allowed them to gain great wealth trading salt, gold and black slaves'."

Devon Douglas-Bowers in
'The Crisis in Mali: A Historical Perspective on the Tuareg People'—Global Research

I came upon the Tuareg people and their somewhat complex culture long before Operation Barkhane, the ongoing anti-insurgent operation in West Africa that was launched in the wake of Operation Serval in August 2014. In fact, my contact took place about thirty years before, while moving by vehicle through the Niger Republic and into the interior of the great Sahel when I first stumbled on a remarkable community of Tuareg craftsmen in Agadez.

This largish city—not long ago the last stop on the overland leg north toward the Mediterranean before Tamanrasset in Algeria—is one of the ancient capitals of Sahara trade. Its links with Cairo, Libya's Tripoli, Algiers and several Moroccan cities go back seven centuries or more. These days tourists dare not contemplate the overland trip, a pity because it was always integral to the romantic lore of a distant corner of historical Africa.

A part of an ancient Tuareg–Berber federation, Agadez sits at the western end of the medieval Trans-Saharan caravan route that linked the city to the salt pits of Bilma, 500 kilometres to the northeast. Not all that long ago these slow-moving, twisting columns composed of between 2,000 and 4,000 camels covered the distance in six or seven weeks, taking salt one way and essential supplies needed for the isolated desert communities the other. They were still at it when I visited Agadez.

For years Bilma was at the top of my 'bucket list', but with AQIM on the move, I fear it will never happen. In any event, trucks have supplanted the legendary 'ships of the desert', which is perhaps just as well as the Ténéré in northern Niger has encroached and soon the pits will be no more. But the region has something that for a long time was of even more interest to me as a collector of African art.

Agadez was always—and still remains—the home of a tiny community of skilled Tuareg craftsmen who fashion beautiful pendants for men and women from silver coins that are hundreds of years old. For 'raw stock' they use Maria Theresa thalers, a silver bullion coin that has been continuously in circulation since they were first minted in Austria in 1741.

There was a time when the thaler—the word eventually translated into the dollar in the 1800s—was the currency of choice throughout much of the Middle East. Every cross these artists design is unique, though they bear little resemblance to anything Christian. Rather, styles are associated with a different region or Tuareg clan group, twenty-three variants in all. The workmanship is unusual and of exceptionally high quality, yet curiously, fine

A former rebel in the back of a 'technical', with a clutch of RPG-7 rockets.

examples were selling for perhaps £10. Nobody would say where the original supply of coins came from or how many had been stashed in some remote Saharan location goodness knows when.

This talented, multifaceted society has its own language, Tamacheq, which is linked to the Berber group. The majority of Tuaregs follow Islam, but laced with traditional beliefs and practices that include the men covering their faces with a blue cloth dyed with indigo: the women are never veiled.

Thus surfaced reports from early travellers of a mysterious and hostile community of 'Blue Men of the Sahara'. The word *tuareg* is an Arabic term that means 'abandoned by God' whereas they like to refer to themselves as 'free men', or in their own language, *imohag*, and they have a wealth of traditions. For instance, the Tuaregs have preserved many of their pre-Islamic rituals. Like many followers of Islam in northern Africa, they believe

Tuareg combatants who have switched sides to fight alongside the French.

in the continuous presence of various spirits (*djinns*) and Tuareg men wear protective amulets that contain verses from the Qu'ran, while the women have great freedom and participate in family and tribal decisions. Descent and inheritance are both through the maternal lineage; indeed several African communities follow this.

Generally, while there are exceptions, the Tuareg approach to strangers verges on the xenophobic and for centuries these people seem to have been opposed to any kind of foreign influence. For as long as there has been recorded history, almost the entire West African Sahel—as well as large parts of the Sahara—have remained strictly no-go areas for European explorers, which is why they gave the French, intent on colonizing eastward out of present-day Senegal two centuries ago such a tough time.

The handful of white men that did that manage to get in and out in the nineteenth century, like Frenchman René-Auguste Caillié and Heinrich Barth, professed to have embraced the Islamic faith. That seemed to work, though some white converts did not survive, murdered because they were believed to have been secret agents of the white infidels on the "far side [north] of the great inland sea [the Mediterranean]". That phraseology alone suggests that they knew very well that an enormous ocean, the Atlantic, fringed the western limits of their own historic expanse.

Of course, after subjugation by the French things did improve and both sides learned, if not to live alongside one another, then, at least, to accept the tenets of their former adversaries, if only grudgingly. One consequence was the number of Tuaregs in uniform through two world wars.

My personal experiences of associating with Tuaregs as finders, fixers and factotums while making TV documentaries were never unpleasant. Almost all the drivers I hired in Mali and Niger were of Tuareg extraction and I found them to be thoroughly decent chaps, though they would never muck in with the crew once the day's work was done.

For all that—and in spite of their disparate traditions—the influence of the Tuareg covers an enormous swathe of arid Africa in the Sahel/Sahara regions. For instance, there are fairly large Tuareg communities that have lived in southern Libya since the year dot and nobody can venture a guess as to why they went there or when.

Muammar Gaddafi recognized the Tuaregs as gritty and resourceful and, more often than not, as relentless fighters. He promoted the careers of many of them in the Libyan army and encouraged and rewarded loyalty both financially and with positions of trust, as well as responsibility. After Gaddafi was killed, his son Saif sought refuge with these people and they took to escorting him across the Sahara between Libya and the southern areas where they controlled large tracts.

What is not generally known is that tens of thousands of Tuaregs served in the Libyan armed forces over several decades. Once they had proved to Gaddafi that they were loyal and trustworthy he, in turn, accorded them the kind of privileges they could never achieve in their own countries in the Sahel. In time they became a significant 'sub-force' that could be depended upon to do the kind of work that other Libyan units preferred not to do, including removing recalcitrant and subversive citizens who threatened to undermine the status quo.

Malian Tuaregs meet with a Red Cross official. (Photo ICRC)

Mali's 'men in blue', a Saharan Tuareg.

This situation had its drawbacks. Obviously, Tuareg soldiers under Gaddafi's direct orders were despised and often regarded with great suspicion by native Libyans. They resented their clout and once the dreaded dictator had been overthrown in 2011, many Tuareg units and their commanders were hunted down and killed, with thousands more arrested and jailed. The number of Tuaregs who died in the post-Gaddafi uprisings will never be known but are believed to be well into five figures.

Finally, with civil war ravaging most of Libya's more settled regions, the survivors were given an option: leave the country and go to your roots or die. Enormous columns of Tuaregs fled south, many to Mali and the Niger Republic and lesser numbers to Burkina Faso, sometimes more than a hundred refugees in a single heavy truck. It was the men among these survivors, most militarily trained, who became the focus of AQIM's new revolution in the Sahel.

Today, a fairly large proportion of an estimated two million Tuaregs throughout West Africa live in Mali, the Niger Republic, Burkina Faso, Mauretania's east, and quite often in northern Nigeria.

It should be mentioned that there are quite a few opinions as to exactly how many Tuaregs there actually are. Some sources talk about a million or less, others about two million or more, but unless there is an impartially organized census—'impartial' because most official bodies in that region do not wish to accept that this might be a more powerful grouping than they would like—we will never know. The generally accepted figure, typically African in context, is 'more than a million and less than two million.'

In Mali this community is well structured along hierarchical grounds, which is important because Tuaregs in that country are allied to three distinct traditional political entities called 'confederations'.

The stomping grounds of the Kel Tademekat community are to be found in the vicinity and toward the north of Timbuktu; the Iwellemeden people live east of Gao and regard Menaka and In Gall in the Niger Republic as their main urban hubs. The third grouping calls itself the Kel Adrar Tuaregs and they are found in areas around Adrar Massif and the city of Kidal.

There are many more sub-tribes that swear allegiance to one or the other of this tribal trio, though, like the wind, this can change if the inducement is enticing enough, usually linked to some kind of military alliance.

Each of the three confederations has its own regent, or in accepted more recent English terminology, paramount chief. These are divided up again into nobility, religious authorities, handicraft or creative workers, and, at the bottom of the ladder, vassals and servants who—still in the twenty-first century—are often little more than slaves. It was pretty obvious during my own visits that some of those doing most of the domestic work were of a distinctly 'lower order' within these scattered societies.

While travelling through northern Senegal, Niger and Mali on several jaunts over the years, I was able to visit an occasional Tuareg encampment in these scattered regions—usually represented by little more than clusters of tents pitched in the middle of nowhere: our drivers knew exactly where to find them. Other times, I was vigorously shooed off the premises. Conditions, I found, were almost invariably grim. In remote areas there would usually be about a dozen people at each little settlement and those present were quite obviously the poorest of the poor. Children were left to crawl about in the pestilential filth that surrounded the tents, many playing host to swarms of flies and just about everybody seems to be infected with something.

Quite often I would encounter youngsters with one or both eyes half-closed from maladies which seemed rampant, trachoma, an infectious disease, being the most persistent and which could be easily eradicated if there was enough fresh water available for toiletries. But there never is. It also explained why so many of the women whom I met were blind in one eye. You can only speculate what happened to the poor creatures that were totally blind because I never saw a single one, though I am sure they were out there somewhere.

Clearly, the infant mortality rate must have been high and, because of the isolation, I doubt whether many of the younger generation had ever seen a doctor.

Worse, to my mind, was the fact that while international aid organizations were well represented in the cities—Bamako, Niamey, Ouagadougou and others—there appeared to be only modest effort made by these groups to head out into the wilderness and try to remedy these conditions. That was then, more than thirty years ago and with AQIM moving across this stretch of Africa there is even less likelihood of it happening today, though obviously there are likely to be exceptions.

Curiously, I was able to establish that many of those people were actually slaves that had been 'bought' in an unofficial (illegal) slave market on the outskirts of Nouakchott, the Mauritanian capital. More to the point, there is no question that the authorities knew exactly what was going on because it was all very much above board and part of the culture. Apart from Tuaregs, this trade involved other rural communities as well. No doubt the tradition extends into other cities and towns, but is kept secreted behind obscure restrictions, which includes asking any questions about it.

In some of these regions, it was Tuareg militants who were among those who first embraced the kind of jihadist ideals that Salafist fundamentalists propagated and which caused Algeria's eleven-year civil war after the French had been pushed out.

It was an unfortunate and catastrophic chapter in the brief post-independent history of this young country's history. Throughout, there were reports of entire villages having been wiped out, usually in concerted night-time attacks that some said would occasionally involve the Algerian army, all misdeeds executed 'in the name of Allah'. As the Algerian

A Tuareg elder greets the French after they have captured the airport at Timbuktu.

movement's religious leaders declared publicly at the time, "those who died were not true followers of the Faith.'

The Tuaregs, while not a prime cause of Mali's problems—ATT saw to that—the community has been troublesome, in large part because it has been consistently sidelined, first by the French colonials and then by the new political order that emerged with independence movements throughout the region. In this regard, one French hack wryly but accurately commented that while the Tuaregs make up only about ten percent of the population, they seem to confidently generate more than ninety percent of the troubles.

The reason for much of this intransigence is basic. For more than a century and a half Tuareg leaders have claimed they have been discriminated against, which indeed, they have. When France ran the show the Tuaregs were often brutally persecuted and, later, they suffered under the rule of Mali's southern Africans, many of whom, even today, resent a people who they regard as foreign intruders in 'their' land. And that irrespective of the fact that the forefathers of present-day Tuareg society were probably drivingly active in the Sahel a thousand years before black Africans moved northward from the coastal regions.

More to the point, some prominent voices in Bamako proclaim that the Tuaregs were at the heart of West Africa's slave trade before it was finally abolished by France in 1846.[1] As many of us are aware, memories in Africa die hard, especially when linked to real or perceived ills.

In the modern period, Mali's problems with regard to its Tuaregs became serious after independence in 1960, with two phases of government interaction with these nomadic people emerging shortly afterward.

Not prepared to be sidelined by Mali's leaders, many Tuaregs gravitated from the semi-desert toward the cities. In almost every case, it was the 'man of the tent' who would make the decision to move and he would gather the family together, pack up and move on, quite often selling all his animals to raise cash, especially when crossing the Sahara northward, usually on trucks. Others went into self-imposed exile moving to several neighbouring states, notably Libya and Algeria, a situation compounded by a succession of droughts, lack of basic facilities, loss of livestock and, because of poverty, appalling living conditions. As a result, there are today many Tuaregs working in Algeria's oil and gas installations in the Sahara as well as in numerous uranium mines, which makes the Niger Republic the fourth-ranking supplier of the metal in the world.

In a major article by Jean-Pierre Olivier de Sardan, published in France only months after Paris interceded in its former West African colony in 2013 a measure of clarity is offered. In 'The Tuareg Question in Mali Today' he suggests that largely discriminatory attitudes of whites toward black people in West Africa began to change after World War II. When these states gained their independence, he wrote, there were many Tuaregs in official positions and thereafter, a vast process of stabilization took place: "Today the majority of the Tuareg have settled and are living in fixed camps, villages, or towns and while they still practise mobile livestock breeding, they are mostly centred on a fixed territory, or make use of herders." Also, says de Sardan, 'the image of the Tuareg as a fundamentally nomadic people is no longer true … they are mixed with other groups everywhere, and the vast majority of the villages are multicultural and multiethnic. Only the extreme north east of Mali, (including the Adrar of Ifoghas, a jihadist and separatist bastion), beyond Kidal, is predominantly Tuareg (but with a limited Arab presence), rather like the Aïr Mountains in Niger." The image of a vast 'Tuareg country' in northern Mali or northern Niger is therefore erroneous, he states.

In Mali today, basic education is dispensed in the Tuareg language, which is systematically taught at primary school in the same way as all the languages of the country. Furthermore, Malians of Tuareg descent are integrated into the elites, political life as well as state institutions, up to the highest levels that include directors, ministers, prime minister and so on. Indeed, under Touré's government, Tuaregs in particular and northerners in general were represented in successive governments. "The image of the Tuareg as victims of specific discrimination in the political sphere of Mali does not correspond to reality," maintains de Sardan.

His original thesis was completed shortly before the present insurgency and since then, he points out, a lot has changed, including the disappearance of jihadist Tuareg groups, the scission of MNLA as well as the emergence of the 'Upper Council of the Azawad'.

What did not change in the thirty years after independence was that a considerable segment of the Tuareg people knew only exile and refugee camps. Return to their countries of origin often resulted in violence and massacres. Also, an intense feeling of exclusion, combined with repression, tended to create a sense of ill-being among the Tuareg, which, bluntly put, translated into the birth of armed resistance.

Early political black rule following independence was responsible for much of it. In Mali, the Adrar-n-Iforas, adjoining Algeria, was integrated in 1960 with independent Mali, then under the dictatorial regime of Modibo Keita, ATT's predecessor. The country's first president followed the policy of forced settlement in this region and the collection of taxes originally installed by the French. Added to this was the daily humiliation of Tuareg chiefs and harassment by officials. All that, compounded by isolation and political marginalization went some distance toward provoking the exasperation of the Tuaregs, forcing them to take up arms, if only to protect themselves. The revolt that followed was countered by ruthless army repression and the massacring of both people and cattle.

All this was taking place with the complicity of Algeria's Ben Bella, like Keita, another Marxist who offered Malian soldiers the right of pursuit of the Tuareg in Algerian territory. Worse, the leaders who took refuge in Algeria were extradited back to Mali to be imprisoned. After repression in Adrar-n-Iforas, the Bamako government ordained this region a military zone.

It was not surprising, consequently, that during the decades that followed—in spite of closer ties between many Tuaregs and other Malian communities—there were five successive Tuareg uprisings and three basic reasons for this dislocation. The first is economic neglect, especially because the north is landlocked and drastically inaccessible: few roads, tracks in very poor condition, etc. In reality, this penalized all population groups in the north, not the just the Tuareg, and things have not improved markedly since. While some northern towns have some basic infrastructure—Kidal has roughly the same facilities as an equivalent town in the Mali's south—the vast rural areas are generally devoid of basic services.

Second, other communities in Mali tend to regard the north as 'inferior'. Bambara, Soninké or Sénoufo civil servants sent to work there, generally see the posting as tantamount to punishment or exile, or as one of them put it, "If you are caught shagging your boss's wife, you will find yourself sitting in an office in northern Mali not very long thereafter." Sadly, southern people often behave with disdain or arrogance toward the autochthones (the aboriginal Tuareg and non-Tuareg), sometimes imposing the Bambara language in their daily interactions with the locals and scarcely trying to integrate.

And last, a strong tendency in public discourse and in the Malian media to build the symbols of Malian identity on the Malinké–Bambara history and language not only persists, but Tuareg culture barely rates mention in the minds of many southern people. Small wonder then that these northerners sought succour in quasi-military and political groupings of their own, followed by a full-fledged armed uprising in 2012.

At the outset, the Malian Tuaregs were gathered within the Popular Movement of the Azawad (MPA), led by Iyad Ag Aghali. It was with this movement that the Malian president, General Moussa Traori, signed an agreement for the cessation of hostilities. After a few months however, the rebellion resumed its armed struggle and the government was toppled the following March. Meanwhile, there were splits within the MPA that caused the formation of the Popular Front for the Liberation of Azawad (FPLA) and the Revolutionary Army for the Liberation of the Azawad (ARLA) emerged. Thereafter, in a move to coordinate the actions of all these tendencies, they joined forces under the Unified Fronts and Movements of Azawad (MFUA).

6. WHY DID FRANCE INTERVENE MILITARILY?

Andy Morgan is one of the leading authorities on what has been going on behind the scenes in Mali because for years he has been going there a lot. He mentions a friend who worked for Al Jazeera telling him "in her honest opinion" what was going on in the north of that West African country "was the hardest conflict to understand in the world." To which Morgan added "even obsessives like myself—who spend more time reading reports and analyses about the crisis or talking to people closely involved—have to admit that more often than not we are enveloped in a sandstorm of supposition and guess work." Morgan is also on record as having maintained that Islamist Tuareg fighters—the men in their indigo robes—are masters of hit-and-run guerrilla tactics, ideal for conditions in the vast Sahara.

Clearly—looking at what took place in Mali from the start of the millennium, and is still going on because the insurgency is far from over—there is a plethora of theories, deductions and assumptions about its origins.

In this almost unbalanced politically correct world of ours, a lot of commentators have been reluctant to lay blame at the door of Amadou Toumani Touré, one of the most

A French squad searches for mines and IEDs in the north.

corrupt and opportunistic black leaders on the continent who originally took power as result of a coup d'état he himself fomented in March 1991. At the time, with the rank of colonel, he was appointed head of the personal bodyguard of the then extremely unpopular President Moussa Traoré, and obviously became a confidant of his boss. Heading what was termed "a popular revolution" he arrested Traoré and took over the country, remaining in power by implementing some fair and some fouler measures for more than two decades. Granted, coups, revolutions, army mutinies had by then become a fairly common occurrence in West Africa since Ghana was first granted its independence in 1957. Indeed, an American magazine even did an article on the topic titled 'Why Are There So Many Coups in West Africa?' adding in its heading that "it isn't polite to generalize but let's face it, West Africa has a coup problem".[1]

Like Sekou Touré's rigid Marxist Republic of Guinea, Mali after independence quickly turned to the Soviet Union for support, though it eschewed Guinea's hard-line communist approach, which included cutting ties with France.

As a young man, Touré (the ATT one) intended to start his career as a teacher but joined the army instead. A promising recruit, he rose quickly through the ranks and after several training courses in the Soviet Union and France, became the commander of the Mali's parachute commandos in 1984. There were several uprising during his tenure, always methodically and most times brutally put down. In this regard he did not hesitate using the country's Mi-24 helicopter gunships to suppress dissent, usually in the remote north where there were few witnesses.

Early morning counter-insurgency preparations near Timbuktu.

That was followed early 2012 by protests within the military of ATT's handling of a revolt in the north, as well as the brutal massacre in the desert where a hundred or more Malian soldiers were slaughtered by radicals. Soldiers and many of their wives accused President Touré of mismanagement because the troops involved did not have enough ammunition with which to defend themselves. The AguelHoc massacre, as it has become known, was something of a watershed in the evolvement of the jihadist struggle for power in Mali. It took place on January 17, 2012, just two months before ATT was overthrown. Rebels from the National Movement for the Liberation of Azawad (MNLA) and Islamists from Ansar-al-Din (Protector of the Faith) as well as AQIM attacked the base which lay close to the frontier with the Niger Republic and the easternmost northern city of Kidal, about which we will hear a good deal later.

The violence, it emerged later, was motivated as part of a much larger Tuareg rebellion to seize all government positions in the north. What set this action apart from a dozen or more rebellions in the past was that about a hundred Malian soldiers were lined up and summarily executed "using al-Qaeda style tactics" that were to become commonplace not long afterward in several countries east of Suez.

What was also clear by early 2012 was that the country had had enough of ATT's political and financial machinations. These involved links with a massive Moroccan drug cartel and included smuggling cocaine and methamphetamines across the Sahara to Europe, the latter through the good offices of his close friend Muammar Gadaffi.

A French Army heading up toward the north of the country.

Which raised another issue during his rule: how is it possible that a Boeing 727 can land in the desert, unload something like ten tons of cocaine into a convoy of pickups and then get torched, all accomplished without local authorities intervening or even raising the alarm? It happened and was one of many drug-related events that have gone into local lore.

Though there had been numerous efforts at trying to halt this trade—coupled to European and American investigative attempts—these always ran into a wall of presidential obfuscation each time these issues were broached in Bamako.

One of the first acts after Touré was deposed was the consideration of charges of treason and financial misconduct against him. By then he was being held in close custody in an army barracks close to the capital. But in the end, nothing happened and ATT went into exile in Senegal in April 2012.

Some interesting observations have been made by Paul Mben, a journalist from Bamako.[2] A man of strong standing in the country, he has had a lot of experience both in his own as well as in adjoining countries. I quote him directly with regard to the arrival in Mali of new extremist groups. He stresses that before the 'Troubles' in his country there were very few religious conflicts. Muslims (who make up about ninety-five percent of the population) and Christians (about one percent) lived in harmony and even in the predominantly Muslim north there are Christian churches: "In the northern part of the Kidal region, on the border between Mali and Algeria, the first extremist group— former members of the Front Islamique pour le Salut (FIS)—arrived from Algeria early 1994. A decade later, former president of Mali Amadou Toumani Touré failed to respond to repeated warnings from the people living in this part of the country about what was termed "emerging extremism".

A French Super Puma and VLRA armoured vehicle deployed to Chad in November 2012.

French troops prepare for an operation.

"By then, he and some of his advisers were implicated in drug and human trafficking. One day, during a meeting in his palace in Bamako, ATT told one of his advisers, referring to the newcomers: 'Those people are Muslim like me. If they don't attack us, we don't have any reason to tell them to go away. They are just preaching the Koran.'"

However, as we have seen, this allowed the extremists to advance their jihad in the largely uncontrolled north. The region became a major traffic avenue for drugs, weapons and people. Meanwhile, the extremists collaborated with Tuaregs on logistics and with Arabs on money-laundering transactions.

Mben continues: "During my stay in Tegharghar, in Kidal province in 2005, I witnessed training camps, Madrassas [Qu'ran schools] and the discreet construction of tunnels. It appeared a very well-organized system, with connections to the capital Bamako. I learnt how those recruited by the jihadists fitted to their specific work needs. I also saw that they had a deal with Djandjawids [fighters from Sudan], Al-Qaida, Ansar al-Sharia, Saharaoui Democratic Republic fighters and from Nigeria's Boko Haram ... The Nigerian rebels had no training grounds or facilities of their own. Consequently Boko Haram was permitted to put its recruits through their paces in northern Mali in exchange for reinforcing their own extremists if and when they needed help." And that is exactly what happened in Kidal and Gao in February 2012.

American writer Yochi Dreazen—he spent more than five years in Iraq and Afghanistan while working for *The Wall Street Journal*, which indicates that he is thoroughly familiar with the kind of conflict that had embraced this corner of Africa—wrote

French support with ground armour in the desert of northern Mali.

an excellent feature on the northern Malian city of Gao for *The Atlantic* in its October 2013 edition. It appeared ten months after the French went in. His article was titled 'The Terrorist Training Ground' and gives us a good idea of how things developed after the Islamists had been driven out of Gao, one of the biggest cities in the north. It was later to become the regional headquarters of the French army and air force after their forces had been deployed in Operation Serval.

Dreazen was circumspect about the eventual outcome, or rather the impasse that followed the exodus of Islamic fundamentalists after they had disappeared and he says as much. Someone he spoke to in the 'new' Gao said that there would be good progress if things stayed quiet, to which he added, "that's a big if."

Mali's central government by then was running Gao, but many locals believed that the jihadists who controlled the city the previous year had melted away into the surrounding countryside "where they are waiting out the French".

The man had a point, though that was five or six years before and, as we head towards 2020—apart from the occasional arrest of suspect AQIM sympathizers and a rare suicide bomb, almost invariably intended for military checkpoints beyond the city gates—things appear to have been going on as before. You still have the usual complaints about corruption and government mismanagement, but those sentiments were, and are still, shared by just about every city in the country, Timbuktu and Bamako included. Gao these days is a big place with almost 100,000 residents. It hosts the largest garrison of government troops in the north, but it took a lot of hard knocks when the jihadists moved south in 2012.

Shortly after a loose alliance of forces that included separatist Tuaregs, Azawad and AQIM had seized Kidal, they covered the 300 kilometres to Gao in fleets of Toyota and other pickup trucks and promptly raised the black and white Azawad flag—which closely resembles that flown by Islamic State—over several buildings in the city. They also erected posters that declared "The Islamic City of Gao". Clearly, they were capitalizing on the country's insecurity following an attempted army mutiny the week before.

The rebels had hardly settled in before the Malian army and air force attacked, using their decrepit M-24 helicopter gunships, heavy weapons and some armoured personnel carriers to good effect to drive them out of the main parts of the city. That ended the fighting, at least for a while. But it was a condition that did not and could not hold.

When the rebels attacked Timbuktu, the last major government-controlled city in the north,

Guiding a Puma down in difficult conditions.

they took it with little fighting, which meant the three biggest towns in the north were theirs in only three days. The speed and ease with which the jihadists took control of the north was attributed in particular to the confusion created in the army's coup, leading Reuters to describe it as "a spectacular own-goal".

Small wonder then that Paris was concerned that things had become unstable in what had previously been regarded as one of the most stable countries in West Africa. The way things were going it could be only a matter of days, not weeks, before the rebel vanguard reached the capital.

For all the media hype, Gao then and today is a place of extremes. Dreazen described it as a sprawl of one- and two-storey mud-brick houses that lacked power lines and running water.

But, as he explains, prior to the revolt it was "home to garish, McMansion-style estates of Cocainebougou, or 'Cocaine Town', a deserted neighbourhood that once belonged to Arab drug lords who controlled the region's smuggling routes for hashish and cocaine but fled fearing reprisals from local citizens who blamed them for the Islamist invasion".

He tells us that the city has few high schools and no universities, yet it houses the Tomb of Askia, one of the oldest mosques in Africa, built in the fifteenth century to honour a regional ruler. For centuries Gao—an integral part of medieval history—was best known as the capital of the ancient Songhai empire that once controlled a region larger than France.

On his visit he was taken by a local man, Hasan Haidara, through the scene of a local battle where there were still splotches of blood on the ground and spent ammunition casings lying around and told that several of the fighters were Arabs. "They were not from Mali," he said emphatically. "They were not from here."

Things moved quickly once the rebels had taken the northern cities, too fast for those closest to the drama as the jihadists silenced every music hall in the region, something which was as much a part of culture as the great African river that flowed through its heart. Then a rebel group showed their verve by capturing the small town of Diabaly, north of Mopti, with a lightning strike that originated over the border in Mauritania, which was remarkable because they had to cover a distance of several hundred kilometres undetected in order to achieve that feat. It was their fast-moving pickup columns with heavy machine guns mounted on their cabs that did it, and the move also underscored the ability of AQIM to cross international frontiers unopposed, almost at will.

There were two military developments in December 2012, the first being the recruitment of 15,000 new recruits for the national army, which was effectively three times the number of troops envisaged for an ECOWAS (Economic Community of West African States) intervention force, yet to make an appearance.

Thereafter, the always-vocal Malian army Captain Sanogo—the man who had organized the coup—went public on the need to launch a "liberation war against evil forces" in the north. Since his army had fled in the face of jihadist advances, he did not explain how he would provide his men with the courage to head back and retrieve the country's honour.

Special force operator aboard a French helicopter heads into action, Mali, 2012.

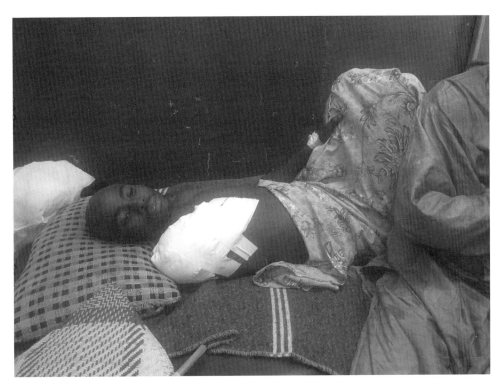

A wounded Malian soldier after his arm has been amputated. (Photo ICRC)

Though the sequence of events that actually pushed President François Hollande to take action is unclear, there is some evidence that the rebel push on Konna and its capture was what ultimately tipped the balance. As the crow flies Konna, a city of about 50,000 people, lies 700 kilometres northeast of Bamako, way beyond a figurative red line past which Mali's military planners (and France) determined the rebels would not be allowed to proceed.

The fighting began when rebel fighters disguised as passengers on a public bus infiltrated the town. The bus was stopped at a Malian army checkpoint on the outskirts of Konna. As soldiers moved in to search it, the rebels opened fire, killing them. Additional rebels poured into the town. After several hours of fighting the Malian army was routed and the survivors abandoned the town to the rebels, reportedly leaving several heavy weapons and armoured vehicles behind. Around twenty-five Malian soldiers were killed.

That done, an estimated 1,200 Islamist fighters advanced to within twenty kilometres of Mopti, a garrison town. The Islamist capture of Konna and offensive in southern Mali triggered the framework of a French military intervention in this West African state in support of the government. The real war had started.

7. OPERATIONS SERVAL AND BARKHANE

Less than a week after France went into Mali to rescue that country from an Islamist invasion that, until then, was doing extremely well, the *New York Times* ran a lengthy story about what was happening in this former French colony in West Africa.[1] The report was one of the most comprehensive to appear about a month after hostilities began. It stated that just as al-Qaeda had once sought refuge in the mountains of Tora Bora, "the Islamic militants now on the run in Mali are hiding out in their own forbidding landscape, a rugged, rocky expanse in northeastern Mali that has become a symbol of the continued challenges facing the international effort to stabilize the Sahara." It acknowledged that the Islamic militants had been swiftly expelled from Timbuktu and other northern Malian towns and, quoting military analysts, an unnamed Tuareg rebel said that might have been the easy part. "Attention is now focused on one of Africa's harshest and least-known mountain ranges, the Adrar des Ifoghas," he declared, adding that a column of soldiers from Chad, versed in desert warfare, had left Kidal, a diminutive, sand-blown regional capital, to penetrate deep into the Adrar.

What caught my eye was a telephone interview from Kidal one of the *Times* writers had with Backay Ag Hamed Ahmed, a spokesman for the National Movement for the Liberation of Azawad. "These mountains are extremely difficult for foreign armies," said Backay Ag Hamed Ahmed and "the Chadians, they don't know the routes through them." In a sense, Ahmed was right, and indirectly, he was wrong, because those remote grottos

A pair of Puma A330 gunships over Mali's northern region in search of targets.

Action at Kidal.

and rocky hills with no roads and few access tracks (known only to the rebels) had been a traditional retreat for Tuareg nomads for almost as long as they had been fighting their wars. But what the rebels did not have and what has turned wars in Africa and most other countries where guerrilla wars have been or are currently being fought—as against Islamic State in Syria, for instance—was close air support. Simply put, the rebels did not have helicopter gunships. The South Africans always maintained during the course of their lengthy insurgent campaigns along the Angolan frontier—and in Angola itself— that a single helicopter gunship was worth two or three hundred well-armed men on the ground, sometimes more. That was underscored not long after that southern African war ended and a few hundred South African mercenaries—with helicopter gunships covering their efforts on the ground—routed two guerrilla armies and helped to end insurgent wars in both Sierra Leone and Angola.[2]

As we are now aware, hostilities in the rocky and remote Adrar des Ifoghas was indeed tough, but it took weeks and not months for the rebels to call it day and slink away into hideaways in the Algerian interior and Libya.

Those hardy few that remained operational within Mali's borders were the "brave ones", as jihadist stalwarts were dubbed by their clandestine supporters. But this segment of the population was small and remains so, restricted principally to northern cities and towns because the majority of southerners want none of their newfangled ideas that abolish music and favour Sharia law.

Aerial view of the Gao military installation after it was taken from the rebels.

Once the impetus of the French military onslaught had subsided, some of those who had fled returned but they tended to remain low-key because Bamako now appreciated the extent of the fundamental Islamist threat and knew more or less what to look for. Still, there were, and still are, those jihadists among them that continued to fight for their version of the Islamic cause. Their sporadic actions against the French army and Mali's security forces are irregular but some of their suicide strikes have been quite spectacular in loss of life and they do make the news from time to time.

They have specifically targeted soldiers and encampments of the Chad Republic—their roadblocks especially—for the simple reason that they are Muslims, like themselves, and should know better than to ally themselves with what was once a despised colonial enemy.

Also, the enemy is shrewd. Once the French moved in, the jihadists covered their pickup trucks with mud and parked them under thick canopies of mango trees to hide them from airstrikes. They stole scooters, which are almost as ubiquitous as the goats on the edge of every village and used them to patrol the town and blend into the population. Meanwhile, they mounted antiaircraft guns on the rooftops of houses, but of course, all that is history now.

With the benefit of hindsight, it is possible to look back on events that immediately preceded the first French air force attacks on jihadist encampments in and around Mali's settled northern regions. What does become manifest is that the enemy was taken by complete surprise, not only by the vigour with which the European-backed onslaught was launched, but that they had absolutely no word of it beforehand. Not even a whisper.

Equally surprised was just about every one of France's NATO allies, the United States especially, being totally in the dark until just before it all kicked off in the second week of January 2013. This is surprising because Washington likes to pride itself on being able to fathom most major events of a strategic or military nature, but not this time round. Just how astonished the Americans were was spelt out in some detail in one of best books on the Mali campaign to appear in the English language three years after Operation Serval had been launched. Titled *The French War on Al Qa'ida in Africa*, the author, Dr Christopher S. Chivvis, specializes in national security issues in Europe, North Africa and the Middle East as well as military interventions, counter-terrorism, and deterrence. He is an associate director of the RAND International Security and Defense Policy Center.[3] Chivvis tells us how, on Friday 11, January 2013, the morning of the first French attacks in Mali, Leon Panetta, the United States secretary for defense in the Obama administration took an emergency telephone call from the French defence minister Jean-Yves Le Drian. The call apparently got off on the wrong foot when Le Drian began by explaining that "the time had come to take action 'rapidly'. Panetta took this to be a request that the United States start the process of considering some sort of joint intervention in Libya.

"'No, Mr Secretary,' replied the French defence minister, 'we are not asking for you to consider an operation. I am calling to inform you that we have just begun one.'" Chivvas says that Secretary Panetta's jaw just dropped. What we are also told is that after the matter had been clarified, "Secretary Panetta's fierce anti-terrorist convictions immediately overcame any initial hesitations and he told his French counterpart 'we're with you, this is a common fight.'"

The airport at Timbuktu became the initial operations base.

An Antonov-124 heavy-lift freighter loading French Gazelle helicopters destined for the Sahel.

Several other countries were also approached for help, including Britain, Germany as well as several African nations that shared Paris's sentiments about Islamist terror. All rose to the occasion, the United States with U.S. Air Force aerial tankers to refuel French planes routed to Mali from Europe.

At the forefront of the African countries that rallied was Chad, already embroiled in a jihadist struggle of its own and with some of the best counterinsurgency forces on the continent.

Though the French military moved with alacrity, it was not a simple matter to neutralize the jihadist threat—not that it can ever be totally eradicated in a part of the world where most people are dirt poor and Allah offers the only comfort, if only in the minds of the believers. Because of poverty, crime flourishes in the region and that makes drug, human and arms smuggling commonplace.

It also emerged that jihadists groups active at that stage were exceptionally well financed, having made fortunes through ransom payments for hostages from Switzerland, Spain, Austria, France and elsewhere. Although European governments have denied paying ransoms, most experts in the region believe it has been quite regular.

Of interest here was the discovery of several factors that indicated foreign support for rebel factions. For instance Algeria was giving large amounts of cash to the Tuaregs, prime movers with Ansar al-Din. There was also Qatari financial involvement. Although it was always rumoured that there were Saudi commanders in AQIM, documents recovered by the French eventually proved this to be true, apparently quite a number of them.

After French forces had overrun the rebel stronghold of Diabaly, it emerged that while most insurgents who held the town for five days were Malian, their commanders were different, local residents said. They were foreigners who spoke Arabic. Six bodyguards protected the most senior commander, a man with a grey-speckled beard and a black turban. The Islamist militant ate Algerian-made spaghetti and Mauritanian-made canned tomato sauce, said one of the residents, adding that Malian fighters served only as his interpreters or brought him intelligence reports. "The Arabic speakers were in charge," recalled Moussa Sangire, 71, a retired soldier who lived next to a house taken over by a group of foreign fighters.

More worrying, though some American pundits liked to play this down while fighting continued, was the amount of hardware that reached Mali from Libya, including light armoured vehicles, artillery, huge numbers of 12.7mm and 14.5mm double-barrelled antiaircraft weapons (also ideal for ground assault) and, more ominously, hand-held ground-to-air MANPADS. Before he was deposed, ATT even confided as much to a French journalist.[4]

Whether AQIM had SAMs or not remains a moot point because they were never deployed by the jihadists, though an Air Algérie passenger plane carrying 116 people—including fifty-one French citizens—on a flight from Burkina Faso to the Algerian capital Algiers crashed as it approached Gao in July 2014. Initially it was said the aircraft was struck by lightning, but the war on the ground below made a proper investigation difficult.

At Gao airport assets are staggered to limit mortar-attack damage.

Operation Serval. (Photo French Ministry of Defence)

French troops at the retaken ancient Fort de Madama in Mali's northwest.

The toughest fighting of the war at the start of Serval came shortly after the jihadists had been driven out of the cities and took refuge in the Adrar des Ifoghas, a long line of black mountains rising above a sea of scrub that are quite clearly visible from downtown Kidal.

Two years after the French went in, the news agency Agence France-Presse reported from Bamako that while the rebels had been systematically ground down, the war was not over. The suggestion among many observers was that the spread of militant Islam had become radically infectious—from the Philippines, through Central Asia and the Middle East to Morocco and numerous Islamic-orientated ghettos in Central Europe— and that it would never be erased.[5]

Based in Mali's inhospitable northern desert, it said, French troops were waging a campaign of attrition against a ghost-like, invisible enemy, a master in the guerrilla art of hit-and-run. The report continued: "More than two years after the French-led Operation Serval routed jihadists advancing on the capital Bamako, armed groups in the area cannot carry out coordinated attacks as they did before. 'Since Serval they have suffered high attrition rates. They no longer have freedom of action on the ground,' the mission's commander, Colonel Luc Laine, told AFP. 'They are scattered, they are watching us, invisible. Their actions are disjointed, unfocused. There is no common thread ... that's what's hard. We're fighting against an invisible enemy,' said Laine, who at home commands the 21st Marine Infantry Regiment, based in Fréjus in the south of France.

"'Their modus operandi is hit-and-run tactics. What is difficult is that we never see them, but we know they are watching us. The risk is that you let down your guard because, as you can't see anyone, you might be inclined to believe that they are not there. So you become less vigilant and therefore vulnerable.

Conditions at some of the smaller airfields in the north are basic.

"They are still there, but in a diffuse, furtive sense. They can no longer lead major combat operations, but they can exploit the slightest lack of vigilance. 'They are smart, they have adapted. They hide their weapons. If they travel by SUV, it is never in a convoy, but one-by-one. It's tricky for us, to distinguish between the trafficker, the terrorist and the [Tuareg rebel]. Some offer their services to the highest bidder. It's a way of life for some people here.'"

There were several major developments following Operation Serval. It was replaced by Operation Barkhane—named after a crescent-shaped dune in the Sahara—with the long-term intention of the campaign becoming the French pillar of counter-terrorism in the Sahel region.

Commenced eighteen months after Serval had been launched, and still running, Operation Barkhane consists of a 3,000-strong French force, permanently headquartered in N'Djamena, capital of Chad. Overall, it has been designed in compass with five former French colonies that span the Sahel: Chad, Mali, Burkina Faso, Mauritania and Niger, collectively referred to as the 'G-5 Sahel'.

According to Le Drian, the main objective of establishing Operation Barkhane was specifically to counter terrorism. With its launch, the aim was "to prevent what I call the highway of all forms of traffic to become a place of permanent passage, where jihadist groups between Libya and the Atlantic Ocean can rebuild themselves, which would lead to serious consequences for our security."

The sprawling French base camp at Gao airport.

An attack against AQIM insurgents.

Airborne operations.

Clearly, France had taken note of what the Taliban had achieved in Afghanistan within a relatively short period before the American-led Coalition forces went in: they do not wish to see something similar taking place on Europe's doorstep, bearing in mind that that Bamako is only four hours by air from Marseilles.

Heading security in this part of the world is what is termed, impressively, the United Nations Multidimensional Integrated Stabilization Mission in Mali (MINUSMA), a peacekeeping mission operating under strict guidelines set by the UN. In fact though, the word 'peacekeeping' might be stretching it a bit because MINUSMA is generally regarded as the most dangerous United Nations deployment in the world. It draws its military personnel from about four dozen countries including near-and-distant neighbours like Burkina Faso, Niger, Ghana and Chad, a number of European countries, the United States and Canada as well as far remoter participants from Asia and Central America.

Operational procedures employed by some of the countries involved have come under criticism in recent years, including the varying and often unsatisfactory levels of training that each troop-contributing country provides which serve to complicate matters. MINUSMA's former commander, Major-General Michael Lollesgaard, highlighted a lack of counter-IED training as particularly significant: al-Qaeda-affiliated militants regularly use landmines and roadside bombs to attack, he said.

On the positive side, MINUSMA is currently the only UN peacekeeping operation with an organic military intelligence-gathering and -processing capability.

As Erwan de Cherisey explained in *Jane's Defence Weekly*, few United Nations missions have been provided with a mandate to conduct offensive operations to enforce peace, and

Checking for mines and IEDs during the early phase of Operation Barkhane.

the majority have strict rules of engagement. That limits the use of armed force to very specific situations, mostly the self-defence of peacekeeping forces.[6]

While MINUSMA has not evolved into an offensive force actively seeking to engage hostile forces, operations undertaken since this announcement have shown a willingness to embrace a stronger posture in countering the activities of armed terrorist groups, which, according to Lollesgaard, represent the most significant threat to the mission and its personnel.

Operation Barkhane.

Counter-insurgency airmobile operations in the southern reaches of the Sahara.

French convoy on the road to Gao, ideal ambush country.

MINUSMA's military intelligence structure is unique in UN history, setting a precedent that could influence future peacekeeping operations by making intelligence capabilities an integral component of UN military deployments. The mission comprises a mix of field units tasked with reconnaissance, human intelligence and air surveillance including an analysis component responsible for centralizing and processing the information generated by these assets.

The initial concept envisaged in 2013 for the intelligence unit was for an HQ at Bamako and three intelligence, surveillance, and reconnaissance (ISR) companies to be deployed in different areas of northern Mali to carry out short- and long-range patrols, and collect imagery (IMINT), as well as human (HUMINT) intelligence.

While the UN agreed that MINUSMA required an in-house intelligence capability, supported by specific force multipliers, including ground reconnaissance units and unmanned aerial vehicles (UAVs), the latter having been first used by the UN in 2013 in the Democratic Republic of Congo as part of the United Nations Organization Stabilization Mission in the Democratic Republic of the Congo (MONUSCO), the concept for a dedicated intelligence unit for MINUSMA was put forward by a number of European countries.

In 2014 a final concept was drawn up, designating a headquarters in Bamako and two ISR units based at Timbuktu and Gao. The HQ, which would exercise control over operational ISR assets and generate the intelligence products required by the MINUSMA leadership to support its decision-making process, was named ASIFU (All Source Information Fusion Unit). This is an additional reinforcement to mission-analysis capacity and came on stream in Mali as a pilot project in 2014.

A French Infantry Fighting Vehicle with a heavy machine gun, similar to those taken from the Malian Army by al-Qaeda.

Technicians working through the night to keep the helicopters operational.

8. THIRD WORLD CHARIOT: THE TOYOTA PICKUP

One of the arresting images to emerge from Mali within weeks of the fighting having started was the number of weaponized pickup trucks about. Better known as 'technicals', these vehicles are a familiar feature in many Third World conflagrations. We first started to see them in Somalia, Chad and Libya years ago, moving about with heavy 12.7mm or 14.5mm antiaircraft guns mounted on the back. Then we saw them with Islamic State east of Suez and, more recently coming out of Chad and into the Central African Republic with the Séléka coalition and the anti-Balaka militias. Mali's AQIM insurrection followed and those jihadists used them with abandon.

Though rarely spotted as far south as Bamako, they were a regular feature of what took place in Gao, Timbuktu, Kidal and elsewhere early in the war. As one source commented, the French army—and most other forces operational in that part of the world—have a great respect for the speed and offensive capability of a *rezzou*, "a long-distance raid by columns of Toyota-mounted fighters armed with heavy machine guns and RPGs".[1]

Speak to travellers passing through from the north and they'll tell you about hundreds more that were formerly operational in the scrub and semi-desert, perhaps an hour's drive away from many of the larger centres. After the French went in, they quickly destroyed anything on the ground that was hostile. The air force had a field day.

Those that belonged to AQIM—many having been driven across the Sahara from Libya—often mounted intimidating hardware that could include the B-10 recoilless rifle, a Soviet-era 82mm smooth-bore weapon. Others boasted the more versatile DShKa heavy machine gun.

There is some dispute as to where these improvised fighting vehicles—Toyota pickups—earned the moniker 'technical'. The term is thought to be short for 'technical assistance' and became a feature of hostilities in Lebanon during that civil war and Somalia in the late 1980s. Pushing these trucks into battle to gain ground or overwhelm an adversary was a 'service' offered by Somali warlords to international aid as well as welfare groups—for a hefty fee, of course—often in the form of convoy protection to ensure that humanitarian assistance in food or medicines reached their destinations.

I went to Somalia often enough in the early days and 'technicals' were always about, including one driven by a youngster who could not have been more than eleven or twelve years old. He swung crazily past us near Mogadishu's fish market and obviously enjoyed the surge of power behind the wheel. With that he was off down the dusty road to terrify others.

There were also a lot of armed pickups around during the civil war in Lebanon, though they tended to avoid the 'Green Line' because high buildings made their drivers vulnerable to snipers. In Beirut's outskirts they would come into their own and just about all the factions had them. The standard procedure was to move them briefly into position and let off a salvo before ducking back behind buildings.

In the 1980s, while making a series of television documentary films on a variety of African countries for the SABC, we would often come across them. In the Republic of Niger, I took a team north toward the Algerian frontier, a long haul by road that took a couple of days. There was no war in Niger then, but we would pass the occasional 'technical' as we approached Agadez and the southern Sahara region.

Between 1978 and 1987, the Republic of Chad and Gadaffi's Libya fought a series of clashes over a significant slice of desert territory known as the Aouzou Strip. As we are told by Kyle Mizokami in the militarily-orientated website www.warisboring.com, that conflict sputtered on for nine years. But what finally turned the tide was a radical stroke of genius, what we would today refer to as an asymmetrical response to the Libyan army and which, indirectly, had an effect on what subsequently took place in Mali. Muammar Gadaffi's military, a strictly conventional force, campaigned in Chad with Soviet tanks, armoured personnel carriers, modern artillery as well as attack jets. By contrast, the Chadian army fielded a ragtag force that could never hope to achieve the same kind of firepower. The Chadians and their French allies knew there was little chance of turning N'Djamena's army into a mechanized force and they didn't even try.

Instead, Chad's military commanders outfitted themselves with 400 Toyota pickup trucks. Modified for sandy conditions, each vehicle could carry half a dozen fighters and as many weapons as they could haul. It worked quite well, as long as comfort

Both Cameroon and Nigeria followed the Malian insurrection with interest.

97

wasn't a concern. All the fighters needed was water, basic food supplies which they would take with them, together with as much ammunition as the vehicle could carry. Many of the trucks had heavy machine guns bolted onto the back, automatic grenade launchers and MILAN anti-tank missiles. Designed by Germany and France to kill Soviet tanks on the guided European battlefield, MILANs could destroy Libyan armoured vehicles at ranges of up to 2,000 metres and the rebels had lots of them.

Light, long range and four-by-four, their vehicles were fitted with extra fuel tanks (as were those used by AQIM). The Chadian pickups were the modern equivalent of Apache warriors on horses and armed with Winchester rifles. The Chadian army, even then a reasonably competent fighting force—with solid French tactical and material support—used a combination of diversionary tactics and raids to demoralize and, quite often succeeded in defeating the Libyans. Columns of Chadian Toyotas would appear in one direction—drawing the attention of the Arabs—and then the main Chadian force would approach from another angle and attack with missiles, destroying the previously invulnerable Libyan tanks.

At the so-called battle of Fada, 4,000 to 5,000 Chadian troops in Toyotas defeated a Libyan armoured brigade, killing 784 Libyans and their allies. Nearly a hundred Libyan tanks and more than thirty armoured personnel carriers were destroyed. Chadian losses were a mere eighteen troops and three Toyotas. Chad scored a similar victory against the Libyan airbase at Ouadi Doum, after which the war sputtered into a stalemate. The Chadian military waited a while and then, made overconfident by their admittedly impressive

A Chadian DIS 'technical' escorts UN workers in December 2011. (Photo UNHCR)

string of victories, went in and counter-invaded Libya. The Libyans eventually beat back the incursion and declared victory, but the Aouzou Strip remains part of Chad. The introduction of Toyota pickup trucks is considered so influential that the last year of that conflict was popularly called 'The Toyota War'.

Special Forces have been using pickups on the battlefield for many years, starting with David Stirling who created a new long-range strike unit in the North African desert with the sole aim of harassing Rommel's forces in a spate of behind-the-lines onslaughts that destroyed dozens and dozens of Luftwaffe aircraft. The unit was given the deliberately misleading name 'L Detachment, Special Air Service Brigade' to reinforce an existing deception of a parachute brigade already operational along the Mediterranean coast. But in fact, Stirling's methods were totally revolutionary within the concept of a modern war.

In the modern era in places like Iraq and Afghanistan, the increased proliferation of Improvised Explosive Devices, or IEDs, forced 'technicals' into the role of military-grade, mine-protected vehicles. And though most of the Americans—and all the British soldiers originally deployed in Helwan—have gone home, Afghan troops still use Toyota 'technicals' in their thousands. So does the Taliban.

In truth, the Toyota pickup should have no place on the modern battlefield though clearly it scored a rather decisive niche early on in Chad and Somalia and thereafter in Mali. It is seemingly the very opposite of a modern vehicle of war: unarmoured, unarmed in its original format, inexpensive and not one of them originated from a billion-dollar development programme run by Lockheed Martin or BAE. Yet, for those very reasons, the

Off to fight al-Qaeda.

Toyota thrives on the battlefields of poor Third World countries, particularly in Africa. The civilian truck seems to have struck an ideal balance between convenience, indigence (or economic reality) and the demands of local terrain.

The proliferation of the light pickup truck in many remote wars is a reminder that people will use what they can lay their hands on to get the job done, and that adaptability is one of the most important traits of any weapon. It is worth mentioning that the Somali terror group al-Shabaab has gone to a lot of effort to propagate their versatility in this field by taking cameramen along with them into battle: invariably their Toyota pickup attack vehicles are involved. These battles that rarely last more than ten or twenty minutes can be viewed on YouTube: certainly, they offer an outstanding understanding why these guerrillas are so effective when they go onto the offensive.

As In Mali, where AQIM liked to strike at what were considered 'vulnerable' static targets, squads of ground forces initiated an action, followed by mounted heavy machine guns driven into the fray with all weapons firing. Cumulatively, it made for a formidable volume of firepower. In some attacks even armour was destroyed or forced to flee, though obviously the defenders resorted to almost none of the established counterattack routines taught by their British or American instructors and which should have kept their positions intact.

In a web report that went viral not long ago, Ravi Somaiya added a corollary to the 'technical' issue. As the war in Afghanistan escalated several years ago, he tells us, American

The Hilux made a spectacular return to combat in the Libyan conflict.

counterinsurgency expert David Kilcullen—a member of the team that created General David Petraeus's original Iraq Surge programme—began to notice a new tattoo on the arms of some of the insurgent Afghan fighters. It wasn't a Taliban tattoo, in fact, it wasn't even Afghan: it was a Canadian maple leaf. When Kilcullen investigated, he says, he discovered that the incongruous flags were linked to what he says became one of the most important, and unnoticed, weapons of guerrilla war in Afghanistan and across the world: the lightweight, virtually indestructible Toyota Hilux truck.

"In Afghanistan in particular," he stated, "[the trucks are] incredibly well respected." So well respected, in fact, that some enterprising fraudsters thought them worthy of ripping off by bringing in inferior substitutes. The imitations, Kilcullen said, flooded the market, leaving disappointed fighters in their wake. "But then a shipment of high-quality [real] Hiluxes arrived, courtesy of the Canadian government. They all had little Canadian flags on the back, which was supposed to reflect Ottawa's goodwill ... and because they were the real deal, and that is how the Hilux is viewed, [and] over time the Canadian flag became a symbol of high quality across the country. Hence the tattoos."

It is not just the rebels in Afghanistan who love the Hilux. "The Toyota Hilux is everywhere,' declared Andrew Exum, a former U.S. Army Ranger and now a fellow of the Center for a New American Security. "It's the vehicular equivalent of the AK-47," he declared: ubiquitous to insurgent warfare and more recently, counterinsurgent warfare. "It kicks the hell out of the Humvee."

Anecdotally, declared Ravi Somaiya, a scan of images from the last four decades of guerrilla and insurgent warfare around the world (the first iteration of the Hilux appeared in the late 1960s) reveals the Toyota's wide-ranging influence. Somali pirates bristling with

Somalia's al-Shabaab and Mali's al-Qaeda both favour the pickup for mobile warfare in remote regions.

guns hang out of them on the streets of Mogadishu. Indeed, *The New York Times* reported that the Hilux is the pirates' "ride of choice". They have also been spotted in Nicaragua, Ethiopia, Rwanda, Liberia, the Democratic Republic of the Congo, Lebanon, Yemen, Iraq and, interestingly, U.S. Special Forces even drive Toyota Tacomas (the chunkier, U.S. version of the Hilux) on some of their deployments.

While former Taliban leader Mullah Omar reportedly liked to charge about in a Chevy Suburban and Osama bin Laden is said to have preferred the Hilux's bigger brother, the Land Cruiser (in the days when he was able to move about). Most al-Qaeda lieutenants, according to a *New York Times* report from the early 2000s, preferred Hiluxes, Even today, says Kilcullen, "you can almost be sure you're dealing with al-Qaeda when you come across them in Pakistan. They use the twin-cab version, because you can carry people and stuff in the back and still be able to mount a heavy weapon."

The Toyota is such a widespread and powerful weapon for insurgents, says Dr Alastair Finlan, who specializes in strategic studies at Britain's Aberystwyth University, because it acts as a force multiplier. It is "fast, manoeuvrable, and packs a big punch [when mounted with] a 50-caliber machine gun that easily defeats body armour on soldiers and penetrates lightly armoured vehicles as well." It is particularly dangerous, he adds, against lightly armed special-forces operatives.

An experiment conducted by British TV show *Top Gear* in 2006 offered something of an explanation. The show's producers bought an eighteen-year-old Hilux diesel with 300,000 clicks on the clock for $1,500. They then crashed it into a tree, submerged it in the sea for five hours, dropped it from a height of three metres, tried to crush it under an RV, drove it through a portable building, hit it with a wrecking ball and set it on fire. Finally they placed it on top of a 100-metre-high tower block that was then destroyed in a controlled demolition. When they dug the vehicle it out of the rubble, all it took to get it running again was hammers, wrenches, and a few dashes of WD-40 lubricant. They didn't even need spare parts.

The Hilux was originally designed, says Kevin Hunter, president of Toyota's design division in California, as "a lightweight truck with big tires on big wheels. It was always intended to be a recreational truck, something that folk could have fun with. They also have a really high ground clearance, which means they're ideal for off-road work".

Jack Mulcaire, a contributor to *War on the Rocks*, one of the best websites of the genre, has his own take on the issue that is certainly well founded in personal experience. During the 2011 Libyan civil war, he helped lead a group of international volunteers that aided and consulted with local rebel councils and units. Titled 'The Pickup Truck Era of Warfare' and posted on February 11, 2014, Mulcaire comes straight to the point: "Let's take a moment to salute a true workhorse. In the world of war machines, the expensive and high-tech items get all the attention and budget—drones, anti-ship ballistic missiles, cyber warfare, and the like ... but, on the battlefields of the twenty-first century, a humble and underrated weapon has quietly showed up these expensive attention-hogs: the pickup truck."

Mulcaire goes on: "The wars of the Arab Spring have brought us into the golden age of the battle truck. Colonel Gadaffi probably thought his vehicle problems had ended after his forces withdrew from Chad, but he would live to be tormented by Toyotas one final time.

The vast Sahara-Sahel region, ideal for the rugged, mobile 'technicals'.

The Mad Max ingenuity of Libya's rebel mechanics, born of desperation during the country's 2011 civil war, surpassed anything that other pickup-warriors in Chad, Somalia, Lebanon and other hotspots had ever come up with ... They quickly became the stuff of legend: the Chinese auto company that produced most of the rebellion's trucks used Libyan 'technicals' to advertise that their trucks were "stronger then war".

The Libyans weren't the best soldiers or the best tacticians, but they were the most innovative engineers. They attached armour plate-mated office chairs with ZPU AA guns, and sawed off the roof to increase the arc of fire for the recoilless rifle in the bed. They produced hundreds of trucks armed with huge S-5 Soviet rocket pods, intended for aircraft. They even cut the turret off of a BMP-1 Soviet armoured personnel carrier and mounted it on the back of a Toyota. Throughout the conflict, he explained, revolutionary militias captured hundreds of tanks and APCs, but even in the war's last battles, 'technical trucks' provided the majority of rebel firepower and transport. Their superior speed, mobility and fuel economy more than compensated for their lack of armour and firepower compared to captured T-72 tanks and BMPs. Some of those same fighting machines eventually ended up in Mali and they performed brilliantly.

9. UNDERSTANDING AQIM'S RELIGIOUS CREDO

To comprehend what it is that motivates the followers of al-Qaeda in the Islamic Maghreb, it is essential to get to grips with the basic tenets of their belief. AQIM is a powerful spiritual, political and military force. As we have seen elsewhere in Africa with Boko Haram in Nigeria and al-Shabaab in Somalia, both of whom have strong al-Qaeda links, they tend, by military means and their own squads of imams who espouse the creed, to achieve results. In the process an enormous number of people are abused, mutilated, maimed and killed. The end result is to force their radical ways of thinking—their ratiocination—as well as their fundamental beliefs, onto societies, like it or not.

The eleven-year civil war in Algeria—it lasted from 1991 until 2002, when the last remnants of the GIA, or Armed Islamic Group had been hunted down—is symptomatic of this trend. The Malian uprising of 2012 was essentially Salafist in origin and AQIM's leaders adopted, almost *in toto*—its fanatical policies. In most cases it was a matter of accept or die. The group responsible for something quite so rigid and uncompromising is commonly referred to as AQIM: officially it is referred to as the Organization of al-Qa'ida in the Land of the Islamic Maghreb (Qaedat al-Jihad fi Bilad al-Maghrib al-Islami), often shortened to Al-Qaeda in the Islamic Maghreb.

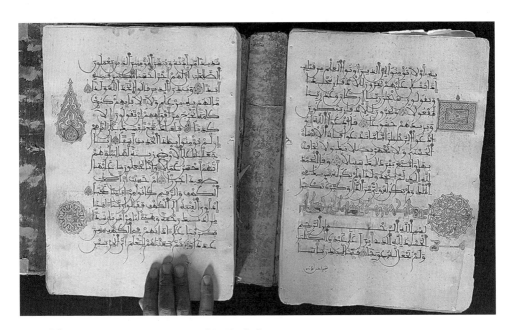

One of the ancient manuscripts rescued in Timbuktu.

While the 'transition'—for want of a better word—started peacefully, the violence that followed soon after they had grabbed most of the towns in northern Mali spun completely out of control. It was abysmally cruel that the majority of people slaughtered by the jihadists were ordinary folk, in their own ways devout and earnest followers of the creed of their forefathers, Sunni Islam of the Maliki School of Jurisprudence.

But that was not good enough for these uncompromising zealots because they tried to eliminate cultural traits that had become part of everyday life in this part of West Africa centuries ago. It started with abolishing music which, frankly, was just plain stupid. The people of Mali, old, young, educated or just plain ordinary, have always shared a great love of music and the arts. In fact, this passion—for that is what it is—is so deep-seated that many Muslims in Mali have distinct Sufi traits. Those who spend time with them will tell you that they are regarded by those who encounter them for the first time as talented, graceful and sensual, three words that are usually abhorred by those who sought to impose their own version of the 'will of Allah'.

In trying to fathom what it is that motivates the average AQIM hardliner, I can do no better than refer to what was written by Antoine Sfeir who is listed on his blog (which can be accessed on Google) as "journalist, political scientist and director of *Les Cahiers de l'Orient*". He deals with some of the issues involved:

Doctrine

Salafism preaches: The return to Islam of the origins by the imitation of the life of the Prophet, his companions and the following two generations; the blind respect of the *Sunna* (Islamic tradition, including the Qu'ran, the *hadiths* and the *sura* chapters).

It condemns: any theological interpretation, especially by the use of human reason, accused of removing the faithful from the divine message; any popular piety or superstition, as the worship of the saints, judged contrary to the oneness of God (*tawhid*); any Western influence, such as lifestyle and consumer society, especially democracy and secularism.

History

The descent of Salafism is sourced to the 'Pious Ancestors' (by the Hanbalite school, the most rigorous of the four Islamic legal schools) which recognizes only the Qu'ran and *Sunnah* as sources of Muslim law and which centuries later inspired Wahhabism, still predominant in Saudi Arabia and Qatar.

Two notions of Salafist following must be distinguished: that of the reformers of the early nineteenth century (Jamal ed-Dine al-Afghani and Mohammed Abduh), who wanted to impose a reform in the quasi-Lutheran sense of the term (the uncluttered reading of texts) and that of the current Salafists, more a blind literature that rejects all innovation (*bida'a*).

The fact is, Salafism is increasingly recognized in the Muslim world and tends to follow the precepts of Islam conceptualized by Saudi theologians. This traditionalist neo-fundamentalism sometimes reveals itself as an intellectual bridge to extremism and planetary *jihad*.

In France, in the 1980s, Salafists were first assimilated to fundamentalists or traditionalists. The 1990s and the Algerian civil war gave a platform to Salafist preachers in the French suburbs, which gain new visibility through the internet.

Islamic halaal prevails throughout the Sahel, as witnessed by this ox being butchered.

Essentially, to those espousing Salafist 'Islamic Revivalism' and 'Political Islam'—rather than the more apolitical popular Islam of brotherhoods found in other areas of North Africa (fanatics who regarded their victims as 'not Muslim enough')—took it upon themselves to destroy and undermine almost everything that went before. Many sacred traditions and ideals were trashed, in the same way that great Islamic literary works—some a thousand years old—that the militants found in Timbuktu libraries and burned because, simply put, they were damned as heresy.

In AQIM's efforts to subjugate Mali, one needs to look for a measure of motivation at Algeria's civil war, not to be confused with the Algerian war against France (often referred to as 'the dirty war' or *la sale guerre*). Fatalities were estimated between 40,000 and 100,000 though nobody knows for sure and there are those who maintain that the final figure is double the upper number. After such a cataclysmic chapter in Algeria's already stormy colonial history under the French, everybody simply wished to forget.

Yet, the events that went before were not forgotten enough by some converts when they turned their attention southward, as they still do today. In truth, not only Mali is affected, AQIM's cohorts are clandestinely operating in a number of other West African countries including the Niger Republic, Burkina Faso, Chad, the Côte d'Ivoire, Nigeria and no doubt, there will be others in the years ahead. Some pundits maintain that because Dakar's leaders recently sought a security linkage with Washington, Senegal is likely to be the next in line to be targeted.

Stephen Ulph, a Senior Fellow with The Jamestown Foundation is one of the pre-eminent analysts of the Islamic World. He has his own view on these issues, well founded because he likes to go to source for his findings, to the point where when visiting Cairo, he sometimes gets into heated debates on street corners that sometimes attract scores of participants. Founder and former editor at Britain's Jane's Information Group of *Jane's Terrorism Security Monitor* and *Jane's Islamic Affairs Analyst,* he has lectured at West Point and delivered two White Papers on the ramifications of international cyber-terrorism before select security committees in the United States Congress. The ultimate polymath, Ulph speaks and reads Arabic fluently, reads Persian and Turkish, which he uses daily in his analytical work and is familiar with some Coptic works.

At the Jamestown Foundation he encapsulated some of the arcane disciplines involved in the study of Islam and published a series of treatises titled *Towards a Curriculum for the Teaching Islamic Ideology,* to which he has given me access.[1]

His thesis, he explains, is fundamental. As he declares, and I quote, "given the demonstrated ability for Jihadism to survive defeat in the field, it would appear obvious that it is at least as important to defeat Jihadism intellectually as well as militarily. Military analysts will argue that the key to success in asymmetric conflicts against ideological extremists has always been not to rely on the physical battle to defeat them but upon the psychological struggle for the hearts and minds of the communities from which they derive their recruits, resources and safe havens."

Timbuktu.

Ulph begins with basics, explaining the term Muslim fundamentalism, itself a complex process. Essentially, he says, the term 'Fundamentalist' implies a category of intellectual process—one of returning to the core fundamental texts of faith for points of reference—and as such is not confined to Islam. "The tendency is one of prioritizing the '*sola scriptura*' instincts of the individual over the historical '*taqlīd*' ('scholarly transmission') heritage of the collective." He then turns to Salafism, AQIM's religious benchmark philosophy and again, it is a complex process. I quote: "The term Salafist mostly overlaps with the term Muslim fundamentalist, but denotes a particular intensification of the tendency, and intentionally focuses upon the legitimizing effect of adherence to a paradigmatic community, that of *al-salaf al-sālih*, the 'pious predecessors' of the first generations of Muslims."

In other words, in the befuddled minds of those doing the proselytizing, just about everything Islamic that came afterwards is invalid, which is why they burn early scriptures and pummel to dust the contents of museums, as their close associates Islamic State in Iraq and Syria were doing until government forces put a stop to that lunacy.

In a sense, we have here a condition that was remarkably handled in the late 1930s by George Orwell who, analogically, spoke out against apologists for Stalin on the Left. He had gone to Spain to fight Fascists and ended up being hunted down by those on his own side who wanted their particular strain of communism to stamp out all alternatives.

Max Rodenbeck, based in Cairo and who has been the London *Economist*'s Chief Middle East Correspondent since 2000 expressed it well when he wrote in a review of

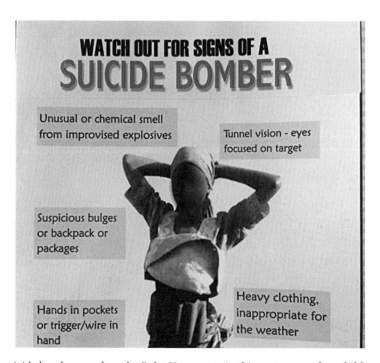

Islamist suicide bombers, such as the Boko Haram one in this poster, are often children.

several books on the Islamic Faith titled 'Islam Confronts Its Demons' in the April 19, 2004 edition of the *New York Review of Books* that "within Sunni Islam, reformers have always chosen one of two paths. Followers of the first trend might be described as literalists, meaning they have sought a return to the letter of Islam's founding texts, namely, the Qu'ran, the *hadiths*, or recorded sayings of the Prophet, and the *sunna*, or recorded doings of the Prophet".

The other trend, he said, "could be called proto-humanist, meaning that they have sought to break free of the texts, reinterpreting them or filtering them in search of a presumed essence that may be more appropriate to temporal or spiritual needs."

One of the seminal observations made by Stephen Ulph in his four-part thesis completed for Washington's Jamestown Foundation is that, quite simply, "al-Qaeda has a pedigree". He goes on to explain that this terror movement has derived much of its power to penetrate into Muslim societies to the fact that it cannot be glibly written off as something alien or external to the broad spectrum of Islamic beliefs. Violent jihadists, maintains Ulph, have not constructed for themselves a doctrine *ex nihilo*.

More to the point, he declares, opponents of al-Qaeda, in highlighting its 'errors', have to concede that its Jihadism, doctrinally speaking, lies deeply embedded within a succession of concentric circles of religious doctrine.

Ulph states that Islamic mainstream is therefore all the more complex a prospect: "The impulse of Islamism, as a fundamentalist movement, is one of 're-authentication', that is, a drive towards regaining the formula that once brought Muslims supremacy but which now has been withdrawn from them."

The mangled corpse of a suicide bomber who blew himself up near a group of Malian soldiers in the northern city of Gao.

Moreover, he states, this doctrinal policy bases itself on a simple interpretative formula: "The political and cultural decline of the Islamic world is not a matter of history or politics. Rather," he maintains, "it is a religious issue—the abandonment of core aspects of the faith through neglect and intellectual corruption."

Ulph goes on: "The solution is therefore to re-establish religious authenticity ... and the protagonists of these re-authentication drives inhabited a spectrum of positions, depending on the degree of compromise they could digest in the cause of the modernization of their fellow Muslims."

But the most intransigent school of thought eschewed compromise as yet one more process of contamination. For these, the inexorable logic of the 're-Islamization' of the Muslim world must be to reverse the equation: to take Islam as the starting point and adjust modernity to its contours.

This, he states forcibly, is the position of the Salafiyya movement, the spectrum of thought from which, ultimately, political Islamism derives. Jihadists, in turn, are a subset of Islamism in its political activism. In doctrinal terms, he tells us, they make claims to define themselves more precisely as adherents to 'Jihadi-Salafism' (*al-Salafiyya al-Jihādiyya*), and although Salafism is far too diverse a movement to be pinpointed as the source and motivator as such of violence, jihadists do make a point of propounding their pedigree as Salafist. This, basically, underlines at the outset the problems in the use of terminology.

The Mopti mosque, situated in the Mopti region, the waist of Mali.

Ulph explains the Salafist concept, the moving power behind some of the revolutionary movements that now hold sway in countries most affected as a consequence of government changes in 2011, following the so-called 'Arab Spring'.

It is his view that in the definition of many groups, the use of the word 'Salafist' appears somewhat liberally used: "This liberal usage is not only the case among Western analysts who may be tempted to think of Salafism as a single school of thought, but also among various shades of fundamentalist movements themselves, since it bestows that all-important aura of authenticity."

Not much precision can be gained from either constituency in using the word 'Salafist' on its own without any further definition, since it gives no clues as to whether it is being used to define a belief or a political/ideological orientation.

The word 'Salafist,' as mentioned earlier, derives from the term used to denote the early Muslim community of *al-salaf al-sālih* or *al-salaf al-sālihūn*, the 'pious predecessors'. While it is correctly seen and used as a broad term to denote 'fundamentalism'—in that all fundamentalist groups look to the past as a model for the future—the term 'Salafist' itself is a far more specific signifier than that. This specificity, says Ulph, is the locus for much internal conflict and lies at the heart of the doctrinal upheaval out of which modern Jihadism has eventually emerged.

As he maintains, "we therefore use the term Salafist here to denote not the common Muslim aspiration to 'imitate the life of the Prophet and the early Muslim Community', but specifically the spectrum of Muslim reductionist schools that set out on a path separate from mainstream Islam, filtering down the heritage of scholarship to its bare, textualist bones, to its least nuanced, least compromising, least organic currents of thought."

Since Salafism is a significant ingredient in the mixture of currents that make up jihadist extremism, being considered by the militant protagonists to lay the cultural groundwork and provide their intellectual mechanisms, it is therefore important to understand the Salafist approach to the problem of Muslim identity in the modern world, and the solutions it has elaborated, if we are to understand the course of events of the second half of the twentieth century. Because the issue of the relationship of Salafism to Jihadism is fraught with polemics and controversy, it will be necessary to spend a moment or two on this.

First, he explains, "it should be emphasized that the term 'Salafism' properly denotes a tendency, one which shares the above inclinations, but does not signify a particular group. It is not, in essence, a new doctrinal phenomenon, but one that has its origins in theological and legal debates that far preceded our time."

The paradigmatic community of pristine Muslims denoted by the term *al-salaf al-sālihūn* is held to comprise the first three generations of Muslims, the companions of the Prophet Muhammad and the two succeeding generations after them (the *tābiūn* and the *taba'at al-tābi'īn*).[2]

Because of the 'pedigree' of the term, it is actually in a broader sense claimed by all Muslims,[3] in that the universal Islamic ideal is to imitate the Prophet and the early Muslim community, just as the entire legal approach is constructed in order to establish rulings that remain consistent with the borderlines set by these 'pious predecessors'.

Given its significance as an intellectual inclination, the historical origin of the use of the term 'Salafiyya' itself is actually difficult to place. The self-styled 'traditionalism' that it represents was only retrospectively referred to as *al-nahj al-salafi* or *al-salafiyyah*, although the term certainly goes back to the medieval period, since it is used by Taqī al-Dīn Ahmad ibn Taymiyya (1263–1328).

Nevertheless, anti-Salafist Muslims today refuse the Salafists' exclusive claim on the term *al-salaf al-sālihūn*, arguing that most Muslims may claim this denomination, as followers of the doctrine established by these and perpetuated by *al-khalaf as-sādiqūn*, the 'truthful successors'.

Their position is that 'Salafism' in the contemporary use of the term, is a latter-day aberration and in any case, the term is not ancient and certainly does not predate ibn Taymiyya.

Bringing us forward a millennium and a half, Stephen Ulph goes on, as we saw before, to say that given the demonstrated ability for Jihadism to survive defeat in the field, it would appear obvious that it is at least as important to defeat Jihadism intellectually as well as militarily.

Military analysts, he reckons, will argue that the key to success in asymmetric conflicts against ideological extremists has always been not to rely on the physical battle to defeat them, but upon the psychological struggle for the hearts and minds of the communities from which they derive their recruits, resources and safe havens.

The prioritization of intellectual defeat is actually underscored by former members of jihadist movements themselves, arguing that while military reverses can be explained away by the appeal to a struggle that is taking place on a long-term scale, ideological justification cannot brook defeat at any point.[4]

The importance of this intellectual dimension has been demonstrated not only by the discovery, by security investigations, of the pivotal role played by radical imams trained in establishing doctrinal underpinnings for militancy,[5] but also by the morale stress to Jihadi sympathizers registered in the wake of the recent 'recantations' by high-profile jihadist ideologues.

Yet while the [West] has dedicated significant effort toward protecting itself against attack from Islamist militants, it has spent far less effort countering the ideology that inspires their acts, or taken seriously radical Islamism's highly focused body of intellectuals and ideologues who tend to legitimize the movement to the Muslim public.

To date there have been insufficient attempts at the level of researchers, intelligence officers and academics to examine the phenomenon focusing on the intellectual tools used by the Islamists themselves, or the arena of debate in which they are making their case. This has led to the development of systems and directions of analysis that base themselves on a number of erroneous points of departure, and which threaten to blunt the edge of any initiative aimed at countering this ideology.

To mount an effective challenge will necessarily require a detailed knowledge of the intellectual terrain and the mental universe of the *mujāhidīn* and how this integrates with its broader target audience.

But while there are some excellent works on the phenomenon of Jihad—its historical development and modern manifestation in Islamist militancy—there are fewer works that set out to describe 'Jihadism' itself, that is, the mindset of its proponents and their view of the world which underpins, and is informed by, their ideology.

Accordingly, Ulph's studies make special endeavours to illustrate the nature and depth of what is a revolution like no other, and elucidate its radicalizing processes. This is done by featuring samples of what amounts to a 'curriculum' of ideological materials, *fatwās*, treatises, books and encyclopaedias, all excerpted and translated from primary sources that are freely available online, and which seamlessly educate, and potentially transform, the reader from armchair *mujāhid* to committed foot-soldier in the cause. Essentially, it is an attempt at mapping a mentality.

To do this, states Ulph, he has intentionally not taken a 'historical development' approach to Jihadism. The point is to present an account of jihadist ideology, not an account of Jihad ideology as it has developed over the centuries, and to avoid miring the reader in a morass of biographies.

As students of Jihadism will know, behind the various manifestations of Islamist radicalism, there is actually a very large degree of agreement on ideological and doctrinal starting points. In the face of commonly held assumptions, scholars of Islamist ideologies are now speaking of more overt 'convergence', conditioned by political facts on the ground.[6]

The ideology of Jihadism, while exhibiting numerous nuances depending on the degree of political engagement in this mix, or the historical role played by theorists, is more consistent than many might believe, simply because the streams all draw from the same sources, and in turn act as tributaries to them. These channels are also porous, in that the sympathizer can wander from one to the other and back without fear of contradiction or compromise.

Therefore his primary purpose is to investigate these common starting points, not the divergences, and seek understanding of the common denominator ideology. Minor differences in emphasis will therefore not be given too much consideration in this study. Instead, he has isolated its operative features and have made reference to any historical development of a feature only where this is relevant to demonstrate its robustness to criticism, on the grounds of its claimed authenticity to the broader Islamic tradition.

The second purpose is to highlight the implications of the ideological ingredients, by illustrating its intellectual depth, internal coherence and robustness in the face of challenge.

Contrary to the observations of some, Jihadism is neither flimsy nor merely a modernist by-product of twentieth century stresses, but rather makes a point of rooting itself deep within the body of Islamic tradition and is very adept at negotiating the seams.

By understanding the potency of its attraction and taking it seriously as an intellectual movement, the hope is that a more thorough groundwork can be laid to the construction of a consistent counter-message to Islamist radicalism, one that will benefit from greater penetration and higher precision.

Such a counter-message cannot be left to deprogramming or de-radicalization initiatives targeted against active militants. Due to the nature of this 'revolution' and its cultural claims to authenticity, the counter-message must embrace the broader communities to which Jihadism seeks to justify itself and make its appeal. These broader communities are no longer their own affair.

An air gunner's view of Timbuktu.

As an ideology with stout and impervious ramparts, Islamist radicalism is highly indigestible and toxic to all environments, irrespective of their cultural affiliation or religious denomination.

In concluding his Part I, titled 'Problems of Perception', Stephen Ulph maintains that in a cause that they define as religious, going 'by the book' is fundamental to the *mujāhidīn*.

They may be selective in the books they read, but read they certainly do. In the summer of 2008 the Saudi authorities released information on the level of interventions they had made against nascent and operative cells in the Kingdom.

One of these was illustrated, showing the haul of literature confiscated alongside the arsenal of weaponry. The names of some of the works were given, among which the famous *Idārat al-Tawahhush*[7] ('Management of Barbarism') of Abū Bakr Nājī, that outlines the ideological and strategic blueprint for accession to power.

The attack on Saudi Arabia's oil facilities in Abqaiq in February 2006—a concerted effort that failed—was accompanied by the publication of a treatise giving strategic and doctrinal justification for the operation. This was al-'Anazī's 'Rule on Targeting Oil Interests'[8] which, significantly, bore the subtitle: 'A Review of Laws pertaining to Economic Jihad'—an emphasis that indicated the essential role of scholarship on religious law.

As 'al-Qaeda in the Arabian Peninsula' relocated from Saudi Arabia to Yemen, their intention to target energy facilities was once again accompanied by ideological backing: al-'Anazī's treatise was duly republished on the internet, as were the online magazines *Sawt al-Jihād* [9] and *Sadā al-Malāhim* ('Echo of the Battles') dedicated to explaining and ideologically justifying the strategic decision.

10. DRONES, REACTION AND RETALIATION

From the start of Operation Serval in 2013—leading into Operation Barkhane during the present phase—counter-terror operations against AQIM and its allies would never have achieved the results they did, and in such a short space of time without the extensive array of air assets progressively deployed by the French and her allies.

Throughout, France has been able to call on an array of aerial-borne assets. These include air force jets operating in Mali as well as out of neighbouring territories together with a variety of fixed-wing transports and helicopter gunships from more than a dozen countries that rallied to the call.

Drones entered the theatre of operations almost from start, first with the earlier generation EADS Harfang and currently with the United States Reaper. The Harfang—*Système intérimaire de drone*—is a system used by the French air force, having supplemented the RQ-5 Hunter. Among its first missions in Mali was filming the French Foreign legion para-drop over Timbuktu, followed by helping to drive AQIM jihadists out of Tissalit.

Initially, a pair of Harfang UAVs—together with several American RQ-9s helping out as an interim measure—were active in Mali, operating from Niamey in neighbouring Niger. These were all replaced by American-built RQ-9 Reaper UAVs. Ordered as a replacement for the Harfang in 2013 they were spotted in service in West Africa in early 2014. A dozen Reapers were ordered by the French, the last scheduled to enter service by the turn of this decade.

These extremely sophisticated aerial devices are hardly lightweights. The Harfang—MALE (medium-altitude, long-endurance) UAV—with a maximum take-off weight of 1,250kg, has a wingspan of seventeen metres and a length of more than nine metres. It operates over target areas at about 200kph.

In contrast, the American MQ-9 Reaper has a payload of 1,700kg, is eleven-plus metres long and boasts a wingspan of more than twenty-one metres, incorporating several features that make it look deceptively like the MQ-1 Predator. Reaper is fitted with six hard points and can carry a variety of weaponry that can include a pair of air-to-ground Hellfire missiles or two 227kg smart bombs (either laser- or GPS-guided). Its effect against an enemy that ranged across thousands of kilometres in some of the most

An airdrop near Timbuktu.

challenging terrain in the world surpassed expectations. As one commentator succinctly expressed it, the performance of the two machines is as different as comparing a touch phone to a smart phone.

The essential data here is that while both drones are geared to twenty-four hours of in-flight autonomy, the Reaper is twice as fast and attains altitudes double that achieved by the Harfang. France, having to dispense with its Harfangs, sold them to Morocco for counterinsurgency operations on the fringes of the Western Sahara.

Operational drone control—as with American drones deployed in the Middle East, Somalia or Yemen—is all manual and handled at an extremely advanced level. Reaper's pilots were originally familiarized with the Harfang and are former aircrew, mostly fighter pilots. Similarly, drone combat navigators are tasked as their operator-sensors. To quote one unnamed authority: "These highly trained staff members are indispensable for several reasons. Deployed in war zones, it is essential that they possess both a military and tactical culture because they work within the confines of operational airspace where armed French fighter jets and combat helicopters are active. Essentially, there are many complex manoeuvres and air traffic issues involved and any mistake might be deadly." They must also be able to coordinate with ground troops, deliver or receive tactical information, and when necessary, 'illuminate' targets for laser-guided weapons, as was the case at the start of Operation Serval. At a hearing before the French Defence Committee of the National Assembly, Chief of the Air Staff (CEMAA), General Denis Mercier detailed the extent of drone missions by declaring that Reaper drones had become "absolutely essential" for the kind of operations in which France now found itself in Africa. "In today's world, in the simplest language, they would be difficult to do without," were his words.

On the runway at Bamako, a pair of French Mirage 2000D jets.

He went on: "Drones enable us to carry out a large number of missions and have contributed to the successes we have achieved in special operations. Additionally they guarantee constant surveillance, indispensable to our operations which allow our forces to follow the activities of terrorist groups in the north of Mali [and by inference, in neighbouring countries]." Interestingly, the general disclosed that the French military was in the process of acquiring light surveillance and reconnaissance aircraft (ALSR).

"Drones and ALSR are persistent means of observation that will consolidate our ability to collect intelligence, indispensable in that war," he declared, adding that only two years after the Reapers were deployed operationally in Operation Barkhane, they notched up 10,000 hours of flying time in what France terms is the Sahelo-Saharan Strip.

Notably, drone operation comes with its own share of problems. According to a *New York Times* report,[1] operators suffer PTSD just as often as among manned aircraft pilots deployed in war zones. Whether this applies to the French is problematic as that nation tends to tackle problems, military ones especially, systemically, as and when they arise.

While the role of the French and other air forces have been dealt with in some detail earlier, there were some notable developments since. For a start, one of the newcomers to become involved in the African campaign was the Airbus A400M Atlas tactical airlifter which some countries have been acquiring as a replacing for the ubiquitous but ageing United States C-130. The first operational mission of an A400, carrying 22 tonnes of freight, took off from Orléans-Bricy airbase and arrived at Bamako in less than seven hours. Its maximum payload is 37 tonnes compared with 19.1 tonnes for the C-130J or 19.6 for the C130J-30. The German air force has also deployed some of its A400Ms on runs to the Sahel; they are a regular feature in most of those regional airports.

Airmen unload a USAF C-130J Super Hercules during a deployment in Agadez, Niger. (Photo US Air Force)

Also, from the start of Operation Serval, the RAF has been involved in airlifts from Europe to West Africa for France's counterinsurgency operations. The latest news here is that C-17 Globemasters from 99 Squadron have been delivering multiple pallets of supplies to both Bamako and Niamey.

Integral to all these operations is in-flight refuelling (IFR). In this regard, the United States has been particularly active with its Boeing KC-135 Stratotankers. France has an air tanker capability but not enough to keep all its planes as well as those of its allies viable. The two main refuelling systems in operation are probe-and-drogue, which is simpler to adapt to existing aircraft, and the flying boom, that offers faster fuel transfer but requires a dedicated boom operator station.

Throughout both operations Serval and Barkhane, airdrops were a feature of supplying ground units with essential needs: fuel, food, ammunition and water. Though these were downgraded once secure road communications between all or most deployments had been established, there were forty-eight airdrops in the Sahel until 2016, all standard parachute drops.

According to Jan Kraak, reporting for *Air International*, the Armée de l'Air carried out its first airdrop by means of an extraction parachute over Madane in the Niger Republic in April 2017.[2] He explained that the newly adopted technique allows for the dropping of larger and heavier loads over target areas "which are often forward operating bases located in remote regions difficult to reach by road".

In conclusion, France's newfound military presence in West Africa, though welcome by most, has had a somewhat mixed reception both in Europe and Africa. Granted, AQIM's wings have been clipped but the situation remains troubled, sometimes extremely so,

A 'Tigre' gunship in a 'brown-out' in the northern Malian desert.

The Harfung drone.

which is to be expected when the majority of the population have almost nothing with which to bless themselves and their families except their religion.

According to the BBC's Alex Duval Smith reporting on August 20, 2017, the war has returned to northern Mali. The desert area had become "arguably more unstable now than at any time since the French intervention in 2013 and the deployment of UN peacekeepers later that year". The 2015 peace agreement failed to settle ongoing turf wars, he declared, and Islamist militant activity spread to the centre of country, which was why the regional counter—the G5 Sahel—was put in place. He went on: "Many Malians say that looking at Mali's problems through a gun sight may be making the country more dangerous."

Quoting Sidy Cissé, a youth councillor for Gao city, it was explained that "every young man wants a gun. Young men are prepared to steal, to kill to acquire a firearm ... they want a firearm so they can claim the right to join the UN-backed demobilization programme and be given a job ... Of course if an armed group offers these same men $500 or $800 to lay a landmine in front of a UN convoy they will do so. They are not acting out of conviction but for the money." Most times it was needed to keep their families alive.

Smith also suggested that diplomats based in Mali as well as senior UN civilian staff had started taking stock of four years of intense international focus on Mali. "The peace deal is just a fig leaf behind which people are hiding ... they actually do not want peace. They want instability so they can continue their shady business," he quoted a diplomat in Bamako as saying.

A Chinook of the Royal Dutch Air Force.

The French took everything with them to Africa, including new Puma engines.

Meanwhile, French Foreign Legion troops have established the makings of a cordon sanitaire in one area in the northern Niger Republic adjacent to the frontier with Libya. The French base of Madama, in Niger's far north, is only about a hundred kilometres from the Libyan border. "It is a grey area from here to the border," a French senior military source explained, adding that "the Niamey government could not control it." In fact, he said, "jihadist groups dominate the west side of the Libyan border while local Libyan ethnic Tubu militia are on the other side."

A BBC report disclosed mid-August 2017 that the French were trying to secure this vast zone to stop Islamist fighters and weapons from moving south and destabilizing their former colonies in the Sahel region, and potentially linking up with the equally radical Boko Haram terror movement in Nigeria.

Postscript

In the final assessment of what seems to have become an endless war against jihadi terror in a largely francophonic region of West Africa, it is axiomatic that France would continue to take the lead. Indeed, it does so with considerable aplomb. That said, there are several serious issues that need to be addressed, some tidily encapsulated by London's *The Economist* in an article published on 3 February 2018 under the heading 'Quicksand in the Sahel' and titled 'UN forces are Finding it Hard to Bring Peace to Mali'. The subtitle—'Peacekeepers are no Substitute for a Competent Government'— is definitive, says the report. Several other issues emerge, the first being that though the warring parties signed a peace deal of sorts in 2015, violence has continued to escalate: there were at least four separate attacks in late January 2018 which killed scores of people. It goes on: "Last year [2017] the UN counted 220 attacks on its operations. That is more than in 2015 and 2016 combined. The peacekeeping mission established in 2013, known as MINUSMA, is by far the UN's most dangerous. It has a force of about 11,000, but 150 peacekeepers have been killed and security has spread from the north to the centre of Mali." *The Economist* stresses that the country's vast desert is not only a breeding ground for jihadism; it is also a trade route that carries consumer goods south and drugs and migrants north to Europe. France has some 3,000 troops in the Sahel fighting terrorists, most of whom are in Mali. The United States has a force there too, as does the European Union (on training missions). Western countries are also paying for a counterterrorism force drawn from regional armies, the G5 Sahel.

NOTES

Introduction

1 Al J. Venter, *Gunship Ace: Neall Ellis, Helicopter Gunship Pilot and Mercenary*, Casemate Publishers, Philadelphia and Oxford, 2011.

2 Al J. Venter: *War Dog: Fighting Other People's Wars*, Casemate Publishers, Philadelphia, 2007.

3 www.telegraph.co.uk/news/worldnews/africaandindianocean/centralafricanrepublic/10565525/Violence-and-reports-of-cannibalism-in-CAR-after-president-quits.html

Chapter 1: The War in West Africa

1 David Blair, 'Beware the Rise of Africa's Own Devil State', *Sydney Morning Herald*, Sydney, January 24, 2015.

2 Dario Cristiani and Riccardo Fabiani, 'Al Qaeda in the Islamic Maghreb (AQIM): Implications for Algeria's Regional and International Relations', IAI Working Papers, April 2011; see also 'Algeria', CIA, retrieved 17 January 17, 2015.

3 Alex West, 'Deadliest Weapon So Far ... The Plague', *The Sun*, January 19, 2009

Chapter 2: Overview of a Desert Campaign

1 International news agencies disclosed on August 3, 2017 that South African hostage Stephen McGowan, kidnapped in Mali in November 2011, had finally been released. Pretoria said that no ransom was paid. He was taken hostage with Swedish national Johan Gustafsson and Hollander Sjaak Rijke, a Dutch citizen. The trio were snatched from a restaurant in Timbuktu along with a German friend, who was shot dead by the militants when he refused to comply with their demands that he climb onto the back of truck.

Chapter 5: The Tuaregs and AQIM

1 Slavery had originally been abolished in all French overseas possessions in 1794, but this lasted only a decade when Napoleon Bonaparte became emperor in 1804 and he reintroduced slavery. It was finally done away with almost half a century later.

Chapter 6: Why Did France Intervene Militarily?

1 John Hudson, 'Why Are There So Many Coups in West Africa?', *The Atlantic*, 17 April 17, 2012.

2 Paul Mben, 'Rebels and extremist stories from northern Mali', *The Broker*, March 8, 2015.

Chapter 7: Operation Serval

1   Adam Nossiter from Dakar and Peter Tinti from Gao, Mali with additional reporting from Eric Schmitt contributed reporting from Washington, and Scott Sayare and Steven Erlanger from Paris, 'Mali War Shifts as Rebels Hide in High Sahara', *New York Times*, 10 February 10, 2013.

2   Al J. Venter: War Dog: Fighting Other People's Wars, Casemate Publishers, Philadelphia, 2007.

3   Christopher Chivvis, *The French War on Al Qa'ida in Africa*, Cambridge University Press, Cambridge UK, 2016

4   Thierry Oberlé in an interview with President Amadou Toumani Touré, *Le Figaro*, Paris, March 14, 2012.

5   'French Soldiers in Mali Stalked by Invisible Enemy', Agence France-Presse, May 30, 2015.

6   Erwan de Cherisey, Jane's Defence Weekly, IHS/Jane's, Couldson, UK, June 7, 2017

Chapter 8: Third-World Chariot: The Toyota Pickup

1   *Doctrine d'emploi des forces terrestres en zones desertique et semi-desertique (edition provisoire): Centre de doctrine d'emploi des forces*, 2013, pp. 101-104.

Chapter 9: Understanding AQIM's Religious Credo

1   Stephen Ulph, *Towards a Curriculum for the Teaching of Jihadist Ideology*, Parts 1–4: Jamestown Foundation, Washington DC 2011/2012. Personal communications; www.jamestown.org/uploads/media/Ulph_Towards_a_Curriculum_Part1.pdf; www.jamestown.org/uploads/media/Ulph_Towards_a_Curriculum_Part2.pdf; www.jamestown.org/uploads/media/Ulph_Towards_a_Curriculum_Part3.pdf

2   They derive this principle from the following hadith: 'The people of my generation are the best, then those who follow them, and then those who follow the latter.' (Bukhari 3:48:819 and 820 and Muslim 31:6150 and 6151). The entire period assumed by this therefore extends from the revelation of the Prophet Muhammad (c. 610) to about the time of Ahmad ibn Hanbal's death (855 CE), each generation understood as approximating some 80 years.

3   The only exception to this would be the Shi'a and Isma'ili Muslims, because their understanding of Islam is based on the assumption that, in addition to the Prophet Muhammad, a series of divinely guided imams who appeared subsequently over a period of two and a half centuries, and one of whom is due to reappear, are also religious authorities. This accounts for why the dynamic of authority in Shi'ism is in some ways less retrospective than that of Sunni Islam.

4   Tawfiq Hamid, speaking at the Secular Islam Summit held at St. Petersburg, Florida, March 4/5, 2007: "If they hear Westerners saying: 'it is culture, Islamism is not wrong', they gain confidence and justification. Because they are convinced that therefore they are not defeated. We therefore need to heavily defeat them mentally too, and encourage this self-doubt and criticism."

5   The point was succinctly made by Louis Caprioli, the former chief of the DST (the French equivalent to the FBI counterterrorism unit), who stated: 'there is always a radical imam behind a Muslim terrorist.' O. Guitta, *Middle East Times*, August 31, 2008, reporting on the banning of Saudi imams preaching in Kuwait

6   See Hassan Mneimneh, 'Are Islamist Doctrines Converging?' and Thomas Hegghammer, 'The Hybridization of Jihadi Groups' *in Current Trends in Islamist Ideology*, Vol. 9, 2009.

7   'The Management of Barbarism' may be considered among the most important texts shaping the Jihadi movement, along with Sayyid Qutb's 'Milestones on the Way', Faraj's 'The Neglected Duty', Juhayman al-`Utaybi's writings, Ayman al-Zawahiri's 'Knights', Sayyid Imam/Dr. Fadl's three books, Suri's 'Syrian Experience', and three books by Maqdisi.

8   Republished online 26 February 26, 2006, two days after the Abqayq attack.

9   Volume 30 of *Sawt al-Jihād* was an edition that turned its entire coverage to the 'oil weapon'.

Chapter 10: Drones, Reaction and Retaliation

1   www.nytimes.com/2013/02/23/us/drone-pilots-found-to-get-stress-disorders-much-as-those-in-combat-do.html?mcubz=0

2   Jan Kraak, 'Air Drops and QRA', *Air International*, August 2017.

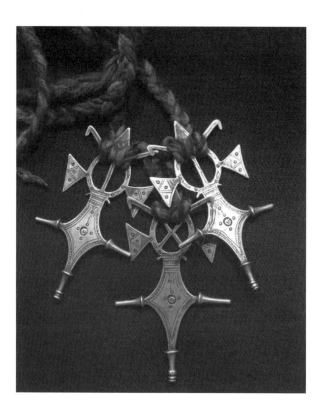

INDEX